FLINDERS ALUMINUM FABRICATION CORPORATION

V.

MISMO FIRE INSURANCE COMPANY

Eleventh Edition

Case File

Trial Materials

FLINDERS ALUMINUM FABRICATION CORPORATION

V.

MISMO FIRE INSURANCE COMPANY

Eleventh Edition

Case File

Trial Materials

Hon. Rebecca Sitterly
Presiding Judge (Ret.), Civil Division
Second Judicial District Court, Albuquerque, New Mexico
Attorney at Law, Albuquerque, New Mexico

Laurence M. Rose
Professor Emeritus and Director Emeritus, Litigation Skills Program
University of Miami School of Law

Frank D. Rothschild
Attorney at Law, Kilauea, Hawaii

Based on the original case file *Flinders v. Mismo*
created by Abraham P. Ordover

NITA®
NATIONAL INSTITUTE FOR TRIAL ADVOCACY

Address inquiries to:
Reprint Permission
National Institute for Trial Advocacy
325 W. South Boulder Rd., Ste. 1
Louisville, CO 80027-1130
Phone: (800) 225-6482
Fax: (720) 890-7069
E-mail: permissions@nita.org

ISBN 978-1-60156-946-2
FBA 1946
eISBN 978-1-60156-947-9
FBA 1947

Wolters Kluwer

Official co-publisher of NITA.
WKLegaledu.com/NITA

ACKNOWLEDGMENTS

The authors would like to thank the following people for their assistance in the creation of this case file:

Abraham P. Ordover, Resolution Resources Corporation, Atlanta, Georgia, for his work in writing the original case file that provides the foundation for this updated version;

Hon. Tommy Jewell, Second Judicial District Court, Presiding Juvenile Court Judge (Ret.), Albuquerque, New Mexico, for his portrayal of the banker John Anderson;

Marjorie Martin, Esq., former Assistant District Attorney, Albuquerque, New Mexico, for her portrayal of Sonia Peterson;

Amy Diaz, Esq., Albuquerque, New Mexico, for her portrayal of Marie Williams;

Brad Hall, Esq., Albuquerque, New Mexico, for his portrayal of Arthur Jackson;

R. Thomas Dawe, Esq., Albuquerque, New Mexico, for his portrayal of the examining attorney in the depositions of Marie Williams and John Anderson;

Lieutenant William A. Dunn, Commercial Crimes Bureau, Sheriff Leroy D. Baca, and the men and women of the Los Angeles County Sheriff's Department for their generous provision of fire scene photographs and video clips of High Temperature Accelerant fires, all of which are used in this case file with the express written permission of the Los Angeles County Sheriff's Department;

Senior Criminalists Vickie Clawson and Phil T. Teramoto of the Los Angeles County Sheriff's Department Scientific Services Bureau for their assistance with the Accelerant Analysis Report;

And a very special thanks to Detective Ed Nordskog, Los Angeles County Sheriff's Department, Arson Explosives Unit (Ret.) and author of *"Torchered" Minds*, a study of serial arsonists, for his invaluable assistance in producing the Ninth and Tenth Editions, navigating the complexities of the National Fire Protection Agency Guideline 921, and for providing excellent film footage of fire scenes for use in this file.

CONTENTS

Case Summary

This civil action was brought by the Flinders Aluminum Fabrication Corporation to recover the proceeds of a fire insurance policy issued by defendant Mismo Fire Insurance Company. Plaintiff's plant was completely destroyed by fire on the night of November 16, YR-1. George Avery died in the fire.

The plant was insured for $10 million. The defendant has refused to pay on the grounds that the fire was the work of an arsonist. It asserts that Arthur Jackson, the sole stockholder of Flinders, conspired with others to deliberately burn the facility in order to collect the proceeds of the policy.

The applicable law is contained in the proposed jury instructions set forth at the end of the case file.

SPECIAL INSTRUCTIONS

This version of the case file is designed for a full bench or jury trial. An "advanced version" for use in an advanced expert witness program, created by Rebecca Sitterly and Karen Lockwood and entitled *Blueprint for Winning: The Next Level*, is available. A "brief version" for use in a very short program of one day is also available. Both versions may be found as appendices at NITA's digital download center. The link is below.

When this case file is used for a full bench or jury trial, the following witnesses may be called:

Plaintiff Flinders:

> Arthur Jackson
> Matthew Korn
> Sonia Peterson
> David Pinkus

Defendant Mismo:

> Marie Williams
> John Anderson
> Janice Jackson
> Donna Olsen

The parties stipulate that Exhibits 20 through 24 are business records as defined by sections 803(6) and 803(8) of the Federal Rules of Evidence, and that witnesses could be called who would identify and testify accordingly. They also stipulate that the video clips of the Flinders, Fass, and Yaphank fires (Exhibits 27 through 29) are actual footage of those fires.

The parties stipulate that Chief Olsen submitted her reports to the State's attorney, but no decision has yet been made as to criminal charges.

All years in these materials are stated in the following form:

- YR-0 indicates the actual year in which the case is being tried (i.e., the present year);
- YR-1 indicates the next preceding year (please use the actual year);
- YR-2 indicates the second preceding year (please use the actual year), etc.

Electronic versions of the exhibits (in color), including videos and a PowerPoint slideshow, are available for download from NITA's digital download center, here:

http://bit.ly/1P20Jea
Password: Flinders11

SUGGESTED TIME LIMITS FOR FULL TRIAL

Voir Dire: 10 minutes per side (5 minutes per attorney when teamed up)

Opening Statement: 20 minutes per side

Witness Examination: 120 minutes per side

Closing Argument: 20 minutes per side

IN THE DISTRICT COURT OF THE STATE OF NITA
DARROW COUNTY

FLINDERS ALUMINUM   )
FABRICATION CORPORATION,   )
)
       Plaintiff,   )
)
       v.   )   No. CV-235894
)
MISMO FIRE INSURANCE COMPANY,)
)
       Defendant.   )

COMPLAINT FOR BREACH OF INSURANCE CONTRACT

Plaintiff Flinders Aluminum Fabrication Corporation ("Flinders"), through its attorneys TINKER, EVERS & CHANCE (Frank Chance), states its complaint against Mismo Fire Insurance Company ("Mismo") as follows:

1) Flinders is a corporation incorporated and licensed to do business in the State of Nita. Flinders is in the business of designing, fabricating, and manufacturing various aluminum components for window frames, beer kegs, and kitchen utensils.

2) Mismo is a corporation licensed to do business in the State of Nita. Mismo is in the business of writing and issuing fire insurance policies.

3) At all times relevant to this action, Flinders owned and operated an aluminum fabrication plant located at 187 River Road, Nita City, Nita 57816.

4) On January 1, YR-10, for consideration paid by Flinders, Mismo issued and delivered to Flinders a fire insurance policy, No. 951946, pursuant to which Mismo agreed to insure the Flinders plant against fire and other perils in the amount of $5 million.

5) Flinders renewed the Mismo fire insurance policy each year following January 1, YR-10. On or about October 1, YR-1, the face amount of the policy was increased to $10 million. The Flinders plant was valued at $10 million, a valuation to which Mismo agreed at the time the policy was increased.

6) On or about November 16, YR-1, the Flinders plant was completely destroyed by fire. The Mismo fire insurance policy was in full force and effect on the date of the fire, and Flinders made a demand on Mismo to pay the full amount of the policy pursuant to the terms of the policy. Mismo has denied Flinders' claim.

7) Flinders has performed all conditions precedent to payment of the fire insurance policy.

8) Mismo has failed and refused to pay Flinders the proceeds of the fire insurance policy, in violation of the terms of the insurance contract.

WHEREFORE, Flinders respectfully requests judgment be entered against Mismo in the amount of $10 million plus reasonable costs and interest on the judgment at the statutory rate, and for such other relief as the court may deem just.

JURY DEMAND

Plaintiff Flinders Aluminum Fabrication Corporation demands a trial by jury in this cause of action.

Respectfully Submitted,
TINKER, EVERS & CHANCE

By: Frank Chance
Frank Chance
Attorney for Plaintiff
411 Main Street
Nita City, Nita 57815
(721) 555-3000

DATED: March 19, YR-0

IN THE DISTRICT COURT OF THE STATE OF NITA
DARROW COUNTY

FLINDERS ALUMINUM FABRICATION CORPORATION,	)	
	)	
	)	
Plaintiff,	)	
	)	
v.	)	No. CV-235894
	)	
MISMO FIRE INSURANCE COMPANY,	)	
	)	
Defendant.	)	

DEFENDANT'S ANSWER

Defendant Mismo Fire Insurance Company ("Mismo"), through its attorneys DIERKER, DIETZ & DIMAGGIO (Ellen Dietz), answers the complaint by Flinders Aluminum Fabrication Corporation ("Flinders") as follows:

I. ANSWER

1) Paragraphs 1, 2, 3, 4, 6, and 7 of plaintiff's complaint are admitted.

2) Paragraph 5 of plaintiff's complaint is admitted insofar as it alleges that the policy was renewed from year to year and that the face amount of the policy was increased to $10 million on October 1, YR-1.

3) Paragraph 8 of plaintiff's complaint is denied.

II. AFFIRMATIVE DEFENSES

4) The policy of fire insurance provides at paragraph 9 that, "This company shall not be liable for loss caused by or resulting from arson where the same was occasioned by the deliberate acts of the insured or any agents thereof."

5) On November 16, YR-1, the insured premises were destroyed by a fire that was deliberately and willfully set by an agent or agents of plaintiff in an attempt to collect the insurance proceeds.

6) Because the fire was deliberately and willfully set by an agent or agents of plaintiff, defendant is relieved of any and all obligations under the policy.

WHEREFORE, defendant demands that the complaint be dismissed and judgment entered in favor of defendant together with the costs of this action.

Respectfully Submitted,
DIERKER, DIETZ & DIMAGGIO

By: *Ellen Dietz*
Ellen Dietz
Attorney for Defendant
Nita National Bank Building, Suite 222
Nita City, Nita 57815
(721) 555-9000

DATED: April 3, YR-0

DEPOSITION OF MARIE C. WILLIAMS
MAY 20, YR-0

MARIE C. WILLIAMS, called to testify on deposition by the plaintiff and having been duly sworn, testified as follows:

My name is Marie C. Williams. I am thirty-five years old. I live at 2242 169th Avenue, Nita City. I am single and have no kids. I live alone and I don't support any relatives. I worked as a bookkeeper and assistant to Mr. Jackson, the president of the Flinders Aluminum Fabrication Corporation in Nita City.

Flinders hired me as a bookkeeper on October 1, YR-10. About five years ago, I also became assistant to the president, Arthur Jackson. I held both positions until August YR-1. On December 1, YR-1, Mr. Jackson fired me. I had worked directly for Mr. Jackson since I joined the company. Mr. Jackson and I had a close personal relationship up until August of YR-1, when he hired Sonia Peterson as his personal aide. After that, my affair with Mr. Jackson ended and so did my position as assistant to the president, but I continued working as a bookkeeper.

Arthur and I had been lovers since YR-4. Mr. Jackson is married and has three children, but he said he was very unhappy and promised to leave his wife. Yes, I knew all along he was married, but I thought that after he left his wife the two of us would work together to build the business.

16	Q:	Ms. Williams, what did Mr. Jackson say to you about his marriage?
17	A:	He said that he was very unhappy at home, and he promised me that he was go-
18		ing to leave his wife. But he never left her, and finally I realized that he had lied to
19		me all along about leaving her.
20	Q:	What was your reaction when you realized that?
21	A:	I was really, really angry with him, and I finally broke off our relationship that fall
22		when he hired Sonia Peterson.

The company employed anywhere from twenty-five to forty manufacturing workers, depending upon the amount of business it had. The workers were assigned to windows, beer keg components, or utensils, and the workforce was designed to respond flexibly depending on which market segment was increasing or decreasing. Mr. Jackson and I administered the company together until Sonia was hired. Flinders employed a separate sales staff of five to eight people for the various aluminum markets we served, but they were not involved in administrative functions. We also employed between ten and fifteen people in the shipping department since most of our products shipped out of town. The sales staff and manufacturing workers always reported directly to Mr. Jackson. While I was assistant to the president, the shipping staff reported to me; when Sonia replaced me, they started reporting to her.

In YR-2, the company had a disastrous year. Losses for the year totaled some $500,000. YR-1 was even worse. Losses for the first nine months totaled an additional $500,000. Bank loans of $2.5 million became due on November 28. In October YR-1, Mr. Jackson attempted to re-negotiate the loans with the lender, First Trust Bank. I participated in those negotiations with Mr. Jackson and Mr. Anderson, vice president of the bank. The negotiations failed. The loans went unpaid pending receipt of the fire insurance money.

At one meeting with Mr. Anderson, Mr. Jackson spoke of the Avery "designs" and the company's plans to get into the airplane parts market with a possibility of expanding into the developing field of space travel that Elon Musk and Jeff Bezos were making news with. Anderson seemed skeptical about the change in direction to airplane parts and requested drawings, market studies, and the like. I don't think Mr. Anderson took the space travel idea very seriously; he didn't ask any questions or pursue that in the conversations while I was there.

The company never undertook any market studies. I recall no negotiations or communications with any airplane parts manufacturer.

Mr. Anderson also requested that we supply the bank with current financial information. Mr. Jackson never asked me to prepare and send such data to the bank, although I kept the information accessible and up to date. I don't know if he, Ms. Peterson, or anyone else ever sent the information.

On July 14, YR-1, Mr. Jackson informed me that if the company didn't pick up new accounts in the last half of the year in our existing products, it would go under. He complained bitterly of financial problems throughout the months that followed.

Sometime in early September, I overheard a conversation between Mr. Jackson and Ms. Peterson She offered to put him in touch with someone named Avery, who, she said, could solve his financial problems. I could see them sitting and talking through the open door of Mr. Jackson's office, which is across from my office. I walked over to that doorway and, staying out of sight, listened to their conversation. My affair with Arthur had ended, and I suspected that Sonia Peterson had replaced me as a lover, not just as an assistant, so I wanted to hear how they talked to each other. I also heard Sonia describe Avery as a "torch" to Arthur. As best I can recall, the exact words she used were something like: "I know a man named George Avery who can solve all of your financial problems. George is a real torch; he could light up this business for you." I heard Arthur say he would like to at least meet the man, and Ms. Peterson said she would text him and see if he would like to come in.

On September 15, YR-1, Mr. Avery came to the plant and met with Mr. Jackson. Afterwards, Mr. Jackson asked me to draw a company check to George Avery for $50,000 and give him both the check and one of our spare plant keys. Mr. Jackson told me Mr. Avery was a tool and die de-signer who would soon be working at the plant to design dies for fabricating airplane parts and that he was going to try to focus on parts that would be the easiest transition from our current products of window frames, beer kegs, and kitchen utensils. I met Mr. Avery, but we did not discuss what his work was going to be. Exhibit 19 is the check I gave to Mr. Avery that day. As I recall, he started working at the plant on October 1.

Also in September, Mr. Jackson contacted the insurance company and increased the fire insurance coverage on the plant, effective October 1. I wrote the check for the increased premium.

I worked late on November 16. I recall Mr. Jackson coming back to the plant at 7:00 p.m. Avery had come in at about 6:30 p.m. One crew was finishing up a rush job. They left at about 6:45 p.m. I was surprised to hear machinery in operation after the last crew had left. I started to go downstairs to check out the matter when I met Mr. Jackson. He was surprised and annoyed to see me there and ordered me to leave at once. I did so. The plant burned down that evening. Avery died in the fire.

1   Q: When did you see Mr. Jackson next?

2   A: It was about a day or two after the fire.

3   Q: What did you say to each other?

4   A: I told him right off that I suspected that he had paid Avery to burn down the build-
5   ing in order to get the insurance money.

6   Q: How did he respond?

7   A: He denied it. He said he didn't do it.

8   Q: What action did you take based upon your suspicions?

9   A: I didn't do or say anything right away, but about ten days later, Mr. Jackson fired
10   me. It was after that that I went to the police and talked to Detective O'Brien, and
11   I told him what I suspected Mr. Jackson had done.

It is true that I no longer care for Mr. Jackson, but that is not why I am willing to testify here. I am telling the truth.

I, MARIE WILLIAMS, do hereby certify that I have read the foregoing pages of my testimony as transcribed and that it is a true and correct transcript of the testimony given by me in this deposition on May 20, YR-0, in the offices of plaintiff's counsel.

Marie Williams
Marie Williams

Certified by:
Ann E. Hall
Ann E. Hall
Certified Shorthand Reporter (CSR)

DEPOSITION OF JOHN ANDERSON
JUNE 2, YR-0

JOHN ANDERSON, called to testify on deposition by the plaintiff and having been sworn, testified as follows:

My name is John Anderson. I am vice president of First Trust Bank in Nita City in charge of commercial lending. I graduated from the University of Kansas in YR-21 with a business administration degree. I then attended Northwestern University in Chicago and received a master's in business administration in YR-17. I received the National Chamber of Commerce fellowship grant in my final year and used it to complete a study of innovative ways to finance new business development in urban areas. My area of concentration while in school was studying the reasons for capital flight from urban centers and methods for revitalizing urban business communities.

I moved to Nita City in YR-16 after completing my fellowship and was hired at First Trust Bank as a loan officer in the residential department. I transferred to the commercial department in YR-15, as my primary interest is in commercial and business lending. I was a commercial loan officer from YR-15 to YR-7. In YR-7, the bank reorganized and established a workout division devoted solely to resolving lending difficulties with companies in default, or at risk of default, on their commercial loans. I managed that division from its inception to YR-6, when I was promoted to vice president in charge of all commercial lending, the position I still hold today. I maintain a direct interest in the workout division, and still engage with customers and staff in devising creative solutions for troubled loans.

In YR-1, Flinders Aluminum Company had an outstanding loan in the amount of $2.5 million. Payment of this amount and accrued interest was due November 28, YR-1. The loan had been taken out five years earlier and was a balloon loan, with interest-only payments due on a quarterly basis. The interest payments had been kept current.

During the month of October of that year, I had several meetings with Mr. Arthur Jackson. On one occasion, he was accompanied by an aide, Ms. Marie Williams. I don't recall that Ms. Williams talked during the meeting. She did not bring any documents with her to the meeting.

During these meetings, Mr. Jackson sought to refinance the $2.5 million loan. His company, he said, was not in a position to make the payment. It had suffered losses of approximately $1 million in the two previous years. The Flinders loan was collateralized with inventory and equipment, but there was no other collateral or a personal guarantee. Over the past two years, residential construction had picked up in the area, so Flinders' inventory of window frames was fairly small. There were relatively greater inventories of kitchen utensils and beer keg components, but nothing that could approach the value of the outstanding loan. Overall, despite the better window frame market, the slumps in the other two markets had resulted in overall losses for the company.

Mr. Jackson said he planned to change Flinders' manufacturing processes over to manufacture of airplane parts. He thought that airplane parts manufacture could take advantage of any equipment or tools the company already had for use in creating its current products. He explained that Brazil, China, and Australia supply the raw aluminum used in the Flinders plant. In his opinion, the company's problems stemmed from the unstable Brazilian market and the continuing supply chain problems in the Chinese market. This left only Australia as a source for most of Flinders' raw supplies, and Australia was besieged with demands from around the world because of the ongoing problems with the other countries. Mr. Jackson thought that if Flinders switched to airplane parts, he could take advantage of focusing on one product line for an industry that had steadily grown. He said the higher prices paid by airlines could offset rising Australian prices, and he could concentrate on Australia as a single or primary supply source. He also speculated that the airline parts business could easily expand into parts for space travel instrumentalities because of the great publicity being generated by Elon Musk, Jeff Bezos, and Richard Branson with their efforts to commercialize space travel. I dismissed the space travel references because that kind of development is simply too speculative at this point.

Mr. Jackson said he had hired an expert tool and die designer to accomplish the switch to airplane parts, and he gave me a copy of the man's résumé. Exhibit 16 is a copy of the résumé Mr. Jackson gave me at one of the meetings. Mr. Jackson wanted to establish a long-term financing plan for Flinders to accomplish the transition to the new product line.

1 Q: What information did you ask for, Mr. Anderson?

2 A: I asked for the current financial data. That included the balance sheet, profit and
3 loss statements, pro forma statements, market analysis. I asked for tax returns.

4 Q: What information did you request concerning the designs?

5 A: I wanted to see a design of the product.

6 Q: What did Mr. Jackson say?

7 A: Mr. Jackson said that they were working on it, and that they would get it into the
8 bank shortly.

9 Q: What was the discussion about the possibility of additional collateral for the loan?

10 A: I didn't ask for additional collateral at that time.

I wrote the loan review committee to indicate that we might become an investor in the new venture if it went forward. The bank refused the renegotiation of the existing loan. Mr. Jackson provided no current financial information.

We took no action on the financing of the new product line. No concrete proposal was ever submitted to us. Nor did we receive the data that we requested.

I, JOHN ANDERSON, do hereby certify that I have read the foregoing pages of my testimony as transcribed and that it is a true and correct transcript of the testimony given by me in this deposition on June 2, YR-0, in the offices of plaintiff's counsel.

John Anderson

John Anderson

Certified by:

Ann E. Hall

Ann E. Hall
Certified Shorthand Reporter (CSR)

DEPOSITION OF ARTHUR JACKSON
JUNE 26, YR-0

ARTHUR JACKSON, called to testify on deposition by the defendant and having been duly sworn, testified as follows:

My name is Arthur Jackson. I just turned forty, and I am married. My wife, Janice, is thirty-eight years old, and we are currently separated. In the past few years, we have had some problems and disagreements, but it all seemed to come to a head after the fire at the plant. In mid-December YR-1, we both agreed that it would be best if I moved out of the family home at 11 Purple Martin Lane, Nita City. I moved into an apartment at 1200 East Gate, Nita City, and I've been living there since. I am the president and sole stockholder of Flinders Aluminum Fabrication Corporation. I purchased the stock of the company in YR-12. Prior to my acquisition of Flinders, I was assistant to the president of Cosgrove Aluminum Company for three years. I am a graduate of Nita University and hold an MBA degree from Nita U.

The Flinders Corporation was housed in a large, old building on the riverfront. The building, made mostly out of wood and brick, was located at 187 River Road in Nita City. The Flinders building had 50,000 square feet of space, spread out equally over four floors. The executive offices, including mine and my administrative assistant's, were in the front part of the building on the second floor. While in operation, the company employed between twenty-five and forty workers in manufacturing, depending on the amount of business we had. We also had a sales force and people who worked in the shipping department. However, the company has no current operations because of the destruction of its plant.

On November 16, YR-1, the company suffered a huge fire. On January 3, YR-0, Fire Marshal Olsen questioned me and implied that I had started the fire or that I had Sonia Peterson and/or George Avery do so. She showed me a company check to Avery in the amount of $50,000. George Avery was a designer of tools and dies. I retained his services in September YR-1, to assist us in changing our product lines to airplane parts. We had been primarily in the business of fabricating window frames, beer keg components, and kitchen utensils. Over the past two years, we had done well in sales of window frames because residential and commercial construction had increased. But widespread publicity about possible health problems with using aluminum in kitchen utensils had collapsed that sector of our business. The sale of beer keg components had flattened and then slumped, and although I tried to research that problem, it is not clear to me why that sector also collapsed. The company had suffered great losses—about $1 million—in the past two years.

19 Q: Mr. Jackson, how did you first hear about George Avery?

20 A: George Avery was recommended to me by Sonia, Sonia Peterson, my administra-
21 tive assistant. She knew of his work from Yaphank and spoke very highly of his
22 designs.

23 Q: Well, what did you do before hiring him?

24 A: She discussed his qualifications with me, and then I interviewed him, and after I
25   interviewed him, I retained him.

I hired Sonia Peterson in August YR-1. We texted back and forth about the first meeting; when she came in, I could tell immediately that she had the skills we were looking for to revitalize the business. I did not check her references, because it was quite obvious that she was skilled and knowledgeable. My instincts about her were right. She told me about George Avery, a master tool and die designer.

I interviewed George Avery and saw right away that he knew what he was talking about with aluminum and parts. We hit it off from the start. He was such a good fit I did not find it necessary to specifically check his references, but he had worked for companies in town that I am familiar with. Avery's office was located on the third floor. He had some excellent suggestions for selling aluminum parts to the airplane industry. We both thought that the airline industry seemed to grow pretty steadily despite occasional slumps, and lightweight strong parts made of aluminum would always be in demand. We were studying that idea in November of YR-1.

The idea that Avery was an arsonist is absurd. He was a brilliant designer. His death in the fire was a terrible tragedy. The $50,000 payment to Avery was simply a basic retainer. If his program was successful, he was to receive an additional $250,000. I knew that Avery was working on drawings and designs, and he told me that when he finished a particular design he would upload it to the Cloud for backup. He designed directly on his own tablet, using design software he personally owned. He said he'd share the designs with me when he finalized each one. There were a lot of possible airplane parts, and we were trying to make use of some of our existing tools and equipment if they could be transitioned to airplane parts. I don't know if he ever got to a finished design on a particular part, but his computer and tablet were destroyed in the fire. We did not have an offsite backup, so his work is probably gone forever. We have been unable to locate or access any location in the Cloud that might have stored such drawings.

Fire Marshal Olsen suggested that Avery had burned the Yaphank plant and was implicated in another fire. I know nothing of these matters and find them impossible to believe.

I worked late the evening of November 16, but late hours were not unusual for me; nor, for that matter, were late hours unusual for George Avery.

10 Q: Who did you talk to before you left that night?

11 A: I talked with George Avery. It was about 6:45 p.m.

12 Q: What did he say to you?

15 A: He said that he was going to work a little longer.

16 Q: Did you say anything back to him?

17 A: No, I didn't. That was normal.

18 Q: Did you see anybody else before you left that night?

19 A: As a matter of fact, I did. I bumped into Marie Williams.

20 Q: What time was that?

21 A: That was closer to 7 o'clock.

22 Q: What did you say to her?

23 A: Well, she doesn't usually work late, and actually I thought she looked really tired.
24   And I said, "Marie, you look beat. You ought to go home."

I wasn't trying to get rid of Marie. We no longer were in an intimate relationship, and things were strained and awkward between us. When I saw her on the stairs the night of the fire, I just thought she looked exhausted and should go. There wasn't any reason for her to be there that late after the last crew had left.

Fire Marshal Olsen suggested that I needed money badly. I had no substantial personal needs, but the company did. At one point, I sent an email to my wife, Janice, asking for a loan for the business. The company had lost quite a bit of money in the last couple of years. In October YR-1, I told Janice that I needed a loan of at least $100,000. She refused to loan the money to me and told me to use my own assets. I told her that my own money was not enough to do the job. I have stocks valued at about $150,000, and my wife and I jointly own our home, which is valued at $550,000. Also, my wife inherited some $1 million from the estate of her father. That amount has been invested in common stocks of large corporations, including IBM, GM, and General Electric. As of the date of the fire, my wife and I were still living together.

Contrary to what the police suggested, I have no women friends. I did have an affair with Marie Williams, but that ended last August. Marie Williams was my administrative aide for almost five years. However, in August of YR-1, I demoted her to her former position of bookkeeper. I did not demote her because I felt hostile to her at all. With the business losses and the strain of the affair, I just thought I needed a completely new direction, at work and personally. A new administrative assistant with new ideas and energy would help me and the business get out of the rut it was in.

In July YR-1, I got an email from Sonia Peterson expressing interest in working for Flinders, and I emailed her back the next day to set up an interview. She said she preferred to text instead of email, and I agreed to communicate with her by text although this was a fairly new thing for me. Exhibit 35 is an accurate copy of our pre-interview texts. I hired Sonia in early August as my new administrative aide. Ms. Peterson is thirty-three years old, and she performed her duties quite well because she immediately got a handle on the finances, the trends in the markets, and the way Flinders works as a company. The police, undoubtedly echoing my wife, contended that I was having an affair with Ms. Peterson. This is not true. Marie was insanely jealous of Ms. Peterson, especially when I returned Marie to status as a bookkeeper only and made Ms. Peterson my administrative assistant. Her jealousy caused me to end our affair. Her baseless charges of arson after Flinders burned down and George Avery died ultimately caused me to discharge her.

My business was really my whole life. Partly because of this, my wife and I quarreled heatedly over the past several months. She claimed I was having a relationship with Sonia Peterson. I denied this, but I knew my wife believed that I was lying. My wife also accused me of being intimate with Marie Williams. Both Marie and I denied that any such relationship existed. Janice and I separated on December 15, YR-1. Our separation was largely due to the Peterson business, but there were some financial considerations as well. Janice complained that she was the only one who always had to pay for any extras the family required. She has custody of our three children: Courtney, who is twelve; Harry, who is ten; and Ambrose, who is six. I should also note that my wife complained that she was the only one who always had to pay for any extras the family required.

Although Flinders had experienced problems, I felt certain that the business would improve this year. My retention of George Avery shows that I was optimistic at that time. His idea was sound. Airplane manufacturers purchase millions of dollars of aluminum parts. Aluminum is both strong and light, and airlines have a constant and expanding need for parts. I was starting to study this issue in greater depth when the fire occurred. I had every reason to believe this idea would turn the company around. I've also been reading about Elon Musk and Jeff Bezos and space travel. They are in the forefront of space travel for commercial and tourism purposes. I thought if we got airplane parts developed in a sound financial way, we could expand to space travel needs and lead the market.

Our losses over the past two years have not been due to poor management at all. In fact, had I not been a good manager, we would have been in much worse shape. We only have three main sources from which to buy aluminum for our manufacturing needs: Brazil, China, and Australia. Brazil is undergoing serious political upheavals, and about two years ago this triggered internal and external mining and shipping problems. Brazil and China had the cheapest products, but with all of the trade problems with China, we started having problems getting shipments we had ordered and paid for. We need between ten days and three weeks turnaround for aluminum orders depending on the product. We need a quick turnround for window frames because that market has actually improved over the past two years. We don't need a quick shipment for beer keg and kitchen utensil uses, as both of those markets have taken a very deep dive in the last two years. I'm not sure why beer keg components are not in demand, but when it comes to kitchen utensils there is a health concern about using aluminum in the kitchen. That market seemed to collapse nearly overnight.

With the constant problems with our Brazilian and Chinese suppliers, we had to rely on Australia to source aluminum. Everyone else in the world was doing the same thing, so Australian prices went up, although they were still able to ship to us in the time promised. Also, Australia has a long history being the leader in aluminum production for the airplane industry. The highest quality of aluminum is necessary, and Australia is a reliable source.

When I was trying to decide what direction to take to try to save my company, switching to airplane parts made good sense. We were already reliant on Australia, and we were continually developing new contacts there. It would have required a major infusion of new capital into the business to retool, even though Avery was going to make as much use as of the equipment and tools we already had for our three product lines.

At the time, the company had a loan with First Trust Bank that we took out in November YR-6. We were required to pay back the entire principal in one balloon payment and had to pay accrued interest every quarter. We were able to keep up the interest payments, and we were never late. The entire principal of $2.5 million plus accrued interest for that quarter was due November 28, YR-1. I personally guaranteed the loan, and we used inventory and equipment to secure the loan, but there was no other collateral. Our inventory had little value in the fall of YR-1. Our equipment was solid, but it was well-used, and I do not think there is much of a market for aluminum fabrication equipment and tools. There was no mortgage on the Flinders plant and land, which was owned by the company, and the value of the land alone was worth several times more than the balance due on the loan.

In October YR-1, I met with John Anderson, vice president of the bank, on several occasions. I sought to refinance the $2.5 million loan soon due and to consider major new financing for the retooling of the plant. Ms. Williams attended at least one of those meetings.

The bank refused to refinance the $2.5 million loan but was prepared to negotiate on the re-tooling matter once it saw Avery's ideas reduced to working designs. I gave Anderson a copy of Avery's résumé. Anderson also demanded that I submit current financials on the company together with market studies and projections covering the new product line.

1 Q: Mr. Jackson, what did you do to meet the bank's requests?

2 A: We were considering what to do at the time of the fire. I needed Avery's designs
3 in order to respond to those requests, and I was planning to contact Boeing and
4 other airplane parts suppliers with those designs. But those designs were lost in
5 the fire.

I wasn't really worried about not being able to immediately meet the balloon payment for the loan, because I knew I had plenty of collateral in the value of the land and the Flinders building, neither of which were encumbered. I did not want the loan to go into default, but I knew that sometimes it takes time to accomplish a larger financial plan. In fact, the loan did go into default, and the balloon payment has still not been made. The bank has still not sued Flinders, and I'm sure the bank would welcome a way to work the problem out without litigation.

I was at home on the evening of November 16 when I received a phone call at about 9:45 p.m. The police told me there was a fire at the plant and I rushed there only to see the building already destroyed. I was told that a deceased male's body had been found in the wreckage, and I told the police that when I had left a couple of hours earlier, George Avery was still at the plant working. They later identified George's body. When I left the plant, Mr. Avery had been up in his office at his drafting table.

The authorities investigated the fire and concluded that it was of suspicious origin. They did not, however, arrest me or anyone else. I am aware that Chief Olsen contends that hydrochloric acid was used to start the fire. That material is regularly used in the fabrication process for all three of our market lines. We always kept five acid-resistant plastic drums on hand, each of which contained ten gallons of the acid. The acid was kept in a storage room on the first floor. No one "started" the fire. I do not know how it started.

The increase in Flinders' fire insurance effective October 1, YR-1, was simply a recognition of the effect of inflation. It was normal for me to increase the insurance coverage on the plant from time to time.

I, ARTHUR JACKSON, do hereby certify that I have read the foregoing pages of my testimony as transcribed and that it is a true and correct transcript of the testimony given by me in this deposition on June 26, YR-0, in the offices of defense counsel.

Arthur Jackson
Arthur Jackson

Certified by:
Ann E. Hall
Ann E. Hall
Certified Shorthand Reporter (CSR)

DEPOSITION OF JANICE JACKSON
JUNE 28, YR-0

JANICE JACKSON, called to testify on deposition by the plaintiff and having been sworn, testified as follows:

My name is Janice Jackson. I am thirty-eight years old. My address is 11 Purple Martin Lane, Nita City. I am separated from Arthur Jackson, who lives at 1200 East Gate. We have three children, Courtney, twelve; Harry, ten; and Ambrose, six. We separated on December 15, YR-1.

I believe that Arthur had an affair with Sonia Peterson. It was not the first time he has had an affair. He had previously been involved with Marie Williams, but he broke off that relationship when I threatened to leave him. I cannot prove he had a relationship with Sonia Peterson, and he denies it. But I don't believe him. He has violated my trust and we just can't live together anymore. I believe we will get a divorce, but our uncertain financial situation has put that on hold.

Yes, the financial situation before the fire was also precarious. You see, I have my own money, $1 million. I inherited $500,000 from my father several years ago. It is invested in large companies, such as Ford, Amazon, and Sony, and it has grown to its present value. I won't touch it since I view it as my children's future, and it is to be used for their college educations and to get them started in life. My husband has his own money and stocks, and he is the sole owner of his company. All of these items are separate. He gave me money each month to pay for the house, clothing, and groceries. I never really knew how much he made, or where his money was kept. He spent it all on the business, and probably his girlfriends.

The business was really his whole life. He loved that business and the people who worked for him. To Arthur, it was a great challenge to stay ahead of the competition and build Flinders into a national firm. He spent more time there than at our house, or with me and the children. Yes, we fought over that too. He always said he was doing it to provide for us, but I told him that he needed to be with the family more. I always paid for vacations with the kids, and the kids and I did the traveling. He was never with us.

I believe that his affair with Marie Williams began in YR-4. She was the bookkeeper at the office. It got to a point that I confronted him in July YR-1 and threatened to leave him. He vowed to break it off and said it would never happen again. The only reason I stayed with him that long, and stay with him at all now, is for the children. I think that he may have stopped his affair with Marie when Sonia Peterson started at the company. He and Sonia were always "meeting" and talking on the phone. Although I can't prove he had an affair with Sonia, it really didn't matter. In fact, we stopped sleeping in the same room (whenever he was home at all) in September YR-1.

In YR-1, around October 4 or 5, Arthur emailed me asking for a $100,000 loan. I emailed him that there was no way I was going to lend him any of my money. He told me that he was going to the company bank and that a bank loan was due soon, and he wanted to use some money to deal with the bank and help the business. I told him to use his own money, or get his girlfriend, Sonia, to help. Exhibit 31 is the email he sent me and Exhibit 32 is my reply.

On November 16, YR-1, the night of the fire, Arthur came home at about 7:30 p.m. We had dinner with the children and then watched some television. Arthur told me that he was a little preoccupied that night because his new design engineer was working late on the new product designs. He had talked about this project several times in the months before, and was really optimistic that his fortune, and our financial picture, would brighten up soon. He was planning to redirect the company into a completely new field and had hired some kind of design guru to help him make this shift. In fact, he said this new man was going to "save his butt." I knew the company had been having a tough time and was happy to see Arthur so enthused about turning things around. At about 9:45 p.m., the phone rang. I answered it. It was the police. They told me that there was a fire at the plant. I told Arthur. He was really shaken. He said that he was going there right away, and he left.

Arthur has not been the best husband or father, but he has never done anything to cause me to believe that he would burn down the business. I'm certain he did no such thing.

I, JANICE JACKSON, do hereby certify that I have read the foregoing pages of testimony as transcribed and that it is a true and correct transcript of the testimony given by me in this deposition on June 28, YR-0, in the offices of plaintiff's counsel.

Janice Jackson
Janice Jackson

Certified by:
Ann E. Hall
Ann E. Hall
Certified Shorthand Reporter (CSR)

DEPOSITION OF SONIA PETERSON
JULY 18, YR-0

SONIA PETERSON, called to testify on deposition by the defendant and having been duly sworn, testified as follows:

My name is Sonia Peterson. I live at 88 Charing Cross Muse, Nita City. I am thirty-three years old. I was employed by the Flinders Company from August YR-1 until mid-January YR-0. I served as an administrative aide to Mr. Jackson, the president of the company. I am presently unemployed, and my only income is my unemployment check, modest child support, and a small disability check for my son Brad. I have been looking for employment in the area of marketing and business and have had several interviews so far, but I have not been successful.

I am a single mother with two children, Mark (fourteen) and Brad (eight). Brad is autistic and needs at-home care, which I am providing at present. I graduated from Nita State University in YR-12 with a bachelor's degree in marketing. Upon graduation, I worked at the Firehouse Insurance Company commercial department for four years. I then moved to the Yaphank Company, where I did marketing with strategic planning for six years when I was let go after a fire. At Yaphank, I oversaw the commercial and industrial storm shutter development.

After Yaphank, I went in with a few partners to begin a consulting business and was the president of the firm. It was called Peterson, Miltown, and Associates and was a venture capital solicitor for start-up companies. Although I wrote excellent business plans for the clients, my partners stole the clients and left me with substantial debts and no medical insurance benefits for my family. I did not sue my former partners, as I did not have funds for an attorney or the costs of litigation. In YR-2, I was able to obtain coverage under the Affordable Care Act for myself and my children, and I am struggling to pay the unsubsidized premium payments.

In July YR-1, I contacted Arthur Jackson, who I had heard was in financial trouble and looking for a turn-around strategy. He got back to me right away. Exhibit 33 is our email exchange. We also texted each other, as shown in Exhibit 35. We set up a meeting the very next week. He told me that if we were successful, I was going to be a shareholder if the company went public. He also told me of some vague concepts about retooling the plant to produce new products, and it was clear that he needed to have a business plan and help for a marketing project. He was focused on changing to aluminum airplane parts, which I did not have experience with, but I told him I would be able to develop a business plan no matter what the underlying product was. Jackson told me that he wanted to raise some capital to turn the business around, but that he didn't want to use the equity in the building and land to recapitalize due to some "community property" issues. He agreed to bring me on board right after our first meeting. I gave him my references from Yaphank, but I don't believe he checked them—at least he never told me he did. After my contacts with Jackson, I texted George Avery to tell him I might be able to help him get work at Flinders. Exhibit 36 is a screenshot of our texts. I had known George from my days at Yaphank, and I had only heard good things about him. I did not know anyone who accused

George of having anything to do with the Yaphank fire, but that's a ridiculous idea. Yaphank was rebuilt, so the accusation of arson doesn't even make sense.

When I arrived at Flinders, I helped draft a business plan, reorganize the files, do a marketing leaflet, and set up PowerPoint presentation packages. Jackson told me to keep the plans from Marie Williams and not discuss them with her, but I didn't really know why. I had the plan, leaflet, and PowerPoint presentations on my computer that was destroyed in the fire. Unfortunately, we did not have a Cloud account or other backup program installed, although we had planned to sign up with Carbonite in December. The company did not yet have the funds to back up all of the computers used in the building.

I was familiar with the financial problems of the company. It had suffered substantial losses in YR-2 and YR-1. These losses amounted to almost $1 million. Moreover, the company owed $2.5 million to First Trust Bank, due November 28, YR-1. Mr. Jackson was negotiating with Mr. Anderson of the bank to handle the $2.5 million loan and the proposed retooling. Those negotiations were not proceeding well, according to Mr. Jackson, although I do not remember the specifics of what Mr. Jackson said about those meetings.

I understand that Anderson wanted projections and market studies done in connection with the retooling. We lacked the expertise to do such studies. I assumed we would hire an independent expert to prepare this data. We hadn't gotten that far when the fire put an end to the plans. I was never asked to, nor did I, send any information to the bank.

1	Q:	Ms. Peterson, what did you do to check on Avery's background?
2	A:	Well, I didn't check on his credentials, but I was familiar with his background.
3		I knew that he was an independent type. He liked to work as an independent con-
4		tractor and move around a lot. In addition to working as a tool and die designer
5		for the Yaphank Company and Fass Meatpacking, he also worked for General
6		Dynamics and McDonnell Douglas and American Motors Company.
7	Q:	What else did you know about his background?
8	A:	Well, I knew that he was a graduate engineer, and that he'd attended Cornell and
9		MIT.
10	Q:	How do you know that?
11	A:	Well, I never checked on his degrees, I didn't call the schools, but I do remember
12		that from his résumé.
13	Q:	Do you know whether Mr. Jackson checked?
14	A:	I do not know. I never talked to Mr. Jackson as to whether he checked on
15		Mr. Avery's credentials.

As I understand it, there are some wild assertions that I was having an affair with Mr. Jackson. Actually, I find him a good man, but unattractive. I also never had an affair with George Avery.

We were friends, and we went to one of Yaphank's company picnics together. He was fun to be around, but we were just friends.

I also have been told that Ms. Williams says I described Mr. Avery as a "torch." Ms. Williams is mistaken. I did not use the word "torch" at all or in any context. Although Ms. Williams says she was positioned outside Mr. Jackson's office when she supposedly overheard this conversation, she still did not hear the conversation correctly, as I did not make that statement. I simply felt that Mr. Avery was a talented tool and die person based upon having worked with him and having heard other people talk about him.

I, SONIA PETERSON, do hereby certify that I have read the foregoing pages of my testimony as transcribed and that it is a true and correct transcript of the testimony given by me in this deposition on July 18, YR-0, in the offices of defense counsel.

Sonia Peterson
Sonia Peterson

Certified by:
Ann E. Hall
Ann E. Hall
Certified Shorthand Reporter (CSR)

Deposition of Matthew Korn
July 12, YR-0

MATTHEW KORN, called to testify on deposition by the defendant and having been duly sworn, testified as follows:

My name is Matthew Korn. I am president of Yaphank Company, which manufactures metal storm shutters.

In June YR-2, George Avery applied to our company for a position as a tool and die designer. I interviewed him and he presented himself well. I was interested in his experience in connection with a new process I was thinking of developing; it was a crimping process to make our shutter edges more user friendly. I checked out Avery's references at McDonnell Douglas, General Dynamics, and Ross Metal. I know Jack Darnell, the division chief at General Dynamics, and I sent him an email asking about Avery in early June YR-2. Jack got back to me the same day saying Avery was a loner but his work was fine. Exhibit 37 is my email to Jack and his response to me. The other references also described Avery as a loner but very talented. I tried to check out his academic references at Cornell and MIT, which were listed on his résumé, but could not confirm them. The people I spoke with said that there was no record of his attendance under that name. But that didn't really matter to me, as his work references were excellent.

Shortly after Avery began his work, we suffered a disastrous fire in our plant. In fact, we were closed for a several months and laid off most of our employees, including Avery. I do know that Avery moved to the Fass plant to work and I used him for two to three months as a part-time consultant after we rebuilt the plant with the insurance proceeds.

Sonia Peterson worked for me from YR-8 to YR-2, but we had to let her go after the fire. She was a good marketing manager. I did not know her well, but only in connection with the business. I do know that she knew Avery while he was with us, as their offices were near each other and they came together to the office cookout in June.

I also am familiar with Chief Olsen. After our fire, she made lots of noise regarding the fire, claiming it was arson. Nothing ever came from her noise, and I told her to either bring me up on charges or shut up. It was only after I threatened to sue her that she stopped talking about our fire.

It is true that our company was having certain financial problems before the fire and that we used hydrochloric acid in large amounts as part of our manufacturing process. I don't see what that's got to do with anything.

I, MATTHEW KORN, do hereby certify that I have read the foregoing pages of testimony as transcribed and that it is a true and correct transcript of the testimony given by me in this deposition on July 12, YR-0, in the offices of defense counsel.

Matthew Korn

Matthew Korn

Certified by:

Ann E. Hall

Ann E. Hall
Certified Shorthand Reporter (CSR)

Exhibit 1

MISMO FIRE INSURANCE POLICY

THE MISMO FIRE INSURANCE COMPANY

FIRE INSURANCE POLICY No. 951946

AGREEMENT between the Mismo Fire Insurance Company (hereinafter the "Company") and the Flinders Aluminum Fabrication Corporation (hereinafter the "Insured").

The policy is to take effect January 1, YR-10.

FACE AMOUNT: $5,000,000

INSURED PREMISES: The plant and property of the insured located at 187 River Road, Nita City, Nita 57816

ENDORSEMENTS:

Face amount: Increased to $7,125,000, January 1, YR-5.

Face amount: Increased to $10,000,000, October 1, YR-1.

[*The standard fire insurance policy is omitted. Clause 9 of that policy states as follows:*]

9. ARSON: The Company shall not be liable for loss caused by or resulting from arson where the same was occasioned by the deliberate acts of the insured or any agents thereof.

Exhibit 2

OLSEN FIELD REPORT

**City of Nita
Bureau of Fire Investigation**

FIELD REPORT

Inv. Flinders Aluminum		Date of Inv. 11/16 and 11/17/YR-1	
Time of Alarm 8:30 p.m.		Date of Alarm 11/16/YR-1	
Fire Location 187 River Road, Nita City			
Type of Building Ind. plant; wood, brick; circa YR-110			
Cause of Fire Hydrochloric acid intentionally released and encountering an open flame.			
Fire Department Nita			
Occupant Flinders Aluminum		Owner Arthur Jackson	
Address Same		Address 11 Purple Martin Lane, Nita City	
		Arrests	
Deaths (1) male; cauc.		Closed	Open XX
Arson Detective Olsen		Police at Scene: Yes	No
		XX	
Preliminary Classification Incendiary			
Remarks:			
HCL stored in large quantities on the premises was used to cause the explosion and fire. The localized destruction and eyewitness accounts of the rapid horizontal spread of the fire support this classification. Obtained video footage of fire from local news channel. Photographs of deceased taken after fire extinguished. This investigator at scene beginning 6:00 a.m. 11/17. Photographs of scene and location of deceased obtained 11/17. Suggest file remain open for further investigation.			
Date: 11/17/YR-1		Investigator: *D Olsen*	
		Donna Olsen, Chief	

Exhibit 3

OLSEN REPORT OF SUPPLEMENTAL INVESTIGATION

CITY OF NITA

BUREAU OF FIRE INVESTIGATION

REPORT OF SUPPLEMENTAL INVESTIGATION

Re: Flinders Aluminum Fabrication Corp., 187 River Rd, Nita City	Reference: Field Report, BRI 202, 11/17/YR-1

Remarks
The deceased found on the premises has been identified as one George Avery, age fifty-seven, of 2318 Crescent Street, Nita City. Cause of death, as established by medical examiner, was from multiple injuries sustained in the explosion. Avery has been investigated previously by this office in connection with fires at the Yaphank Co. and Fass Meatpacking Co. This investigator conducted both investigations at the time of the fires, and I have reviewed the videotape footage of the Yaphank fire and the Fass fire, which I had obtained from a local news channel and stored in the archives of our offices. The video footage of the Flinders fire compared to the video footage of the Yaphank and Fass fires indicates similarities in flame color, smoke color, and flame reaction to water. Avery had been employed by Yaphank as a designer of metal fittings for shutters. The fire occurred two weeks after his initial employment. Although the Yaphank fire was likely arson, there was insufficient evidence upon which to base an arrest. The Yaphank plant was rebuilt following the fire. Avery was re-employed by them on a part-time basis for several months. The Fass fire was also likely caused by arson. Mr. Avery was a paid consultant to Fass. He was retained by them six weeks prior to the fire. The Fass fire was caused by the explosion of HCl, apparently ignited by a mixture of calcium hypochlorite with a common hair shampoo. Oxidation within minutes caused a hot fire which likely ignited the HCl. The company went out of business following the fire. This could have been the setup at Flinders. The traces of the igniter in this case were likely washed away by the fire hoses. However, it appears that one of the machines in the shop had been operating just prior to the fire. HCl combining with hot metal can create an explosive situation.

Date: 11/27/YR-1	Investigator: *D Olsen* Donna Olsen, Chief
	Form BFI 204

Exhibit 4

OLSEN BUREAU REPORT

CITY OF NITA

BUREAU OF FIRE INVESTIGATION

REPORT

Requesting Party	Investigator
Detective O'Brien, Nita City Police Department	Chief Fire Marshal Olsen Bureau of Fire Investigation
Date December 18, YR-1	**Subject** Report of fire occurring night of November 16, YR-1, at an industrial plant located at 187 River Road, Nita City, owned by Flinders Aluminum Corporation

BUILDING DESCRIPTION:

The fire occurred at an industrial plant. The building was four stories high, constructed of wood and brick, approximately 50,000 square feet overall and built in YR-93. The building contained an inventory of aluminum products.

DESCRIPTION OF FIRE:

The fire occurred on November 16, YR-1, at approximately 8:00 p.m. The fire was discovered by Alison Smith, who was passing by the plant on the way home from visiting a friend. Ms. Smith contacted the Nita City Fire Department at 8:30 p.m. Four units responded to the fire and arrived at the scene at 8:36 p.m.

The fire was of considerable size at the time the first firetrucks arrived at the scene. The smoke was reddish brown and was accompanied by large flames. The fire was large and spreading in a horizontal direction at a rapid speed. It took five hours, an unusually long time, to bring the fire under control. The flames became brighter and changed color when hit with a stream of water from a hose. An inspection of the debris indicated that there was one independent origin of the fire.

DAMAGE:

The building was almost entirely destroyed. Only one section of the northwest wall of the building was left standing. The fire caused one fatality. This individual was identified as George Avery, a white male, approximately fifty-seven years old.

ADDITIONAL FINDINGS:

A chemical analysis of the ashes revealed the presence of hydrochloric acid (HCl). An examination of the remaining structure showed that the windows either had been open or were blown out.

My investigation was conducted per the NFPA 921 Guide for Fire and Explosion Investigations. I ruled out the usual accidental causes. Accidental fires involve those for which the proven cause does not involve an intentional human act to ignite or spread the fire. The point of origin was a large combination storeroom and machine shop on the first floor of the building. Analysis of the debris, burn patterns, and damage indicated a "hot spot" in that location and that an explosion had taken place.

I have inspected these premises many times in the course of fire prevention duties. No faulty electrical wiring or motors were found. No heating devices were located near the point of origin. Machines used in coating the aluminum were in the area and apparently had been in use up until shortly before the fire. These machines were equipped with timer starting devices and were capable of being preset to operate automatically.

Hydrochloric acid is not flammable in and of itself. However, under certain conditions it is highly explosive. These conditions would have to have been intentionally created for ignition of the instant fire.

The proper storage of hydrochloric acid is imperative. Many materials prove unsuitable containers because hydrochloric acid is so highly corrosive. The choice of container is dependent upon the quantity of acid to be stored. When a large quantity of hydrochloric acid (such as 10,000 gallons) is to be stored, then the proper container would be a plastic or rubber-lined steel tank. This combination would have the structural strength of steel and the nonreactive nature of rubber or plastic. When a smaller quantity of hydrochloric acid (such as fifty gallons) is stored, a plastic drum is recommended. Because hydrochloric acid may contain traces of hydrofluoric acid, which attacks fiberglass, as a safety measure a container of fiberglass lined with plastic is not recommended.

When a plastic container or liner is used for storage, the hydrochloric acid cannot compromise the integrity of the plastic and leak out of the container. This is because plastic is chemically inert to the acid. Glass could also be used, but problems arise with the tendency for glass to break and the difficulty of repair. An acid leak would occur if the container was ruptured (by a forklift, for instance), if the container was faulty, if the container was sabotaged, or if the wrong drum was used.

Serious problems may arise if hydrochloric acid is improperly stored and leaks out of its container. If the acid contacts a ferrous metal, such as steel, then hydrogen is generated. Hydrogen is an explosive gas. The chemical formula of this reaction is:

$$2HCl + Fe \Rightarrow FeCl_2 + H_2$$
$$\text{(L) (S) (S) (G)}$$
$$\text{(L) = liquid; (S) = solid; (G) = gas}$$

Whereas hydrochloric acid is not in itself explosive, if it contacts steel it will release hydrogen. If the hydrogen encounters an ignition source, an explosion will occur.

CAUSE OF FIRE:

The reddish-brown color of the smoke, together with the large flames, indicates that substances containing nitrocellulose fiber, sulfur, or sulfuric, nitric, or hydrochloric acid were burning. The fact that flames burned brighter and changed color when hit with water is another indication that an accelerant was used. Difficulty in extinguishing the fire also points to the use of an accelerant. A chemical analysis of the ashes showed that hydrochloric acid, an explosive substance when combined with hot metal, in fact was burning. When HCl comes in contact with ferrous metals, hydrogen is released, and when hydrogen is combined with air, it may cause an explosive situation. Although hydrochloric acid is normally present in the plant, scarring of the concrete floor plus chemical analysis showed that an unusually large amount was located at the point of origin of the fire. Moreover, the magnitude of the fire and its rapid spreading indicate that several hundred gallons of the acid likely were splashed about the source of the fire. Normally, a plant of this type and size would maintain a supply of approximately fifty gallons of hydrochloric acid for cleaning purposes. This would likely be stored in one place. Analysis of the debris indicates an explosion at the point of origin, likely caused by a time release igniter, possibly the preset timer of one of the machines, or calcium hypochlorite mixed with shampoo.

The large flames are an indication that the fire was well ventilated. Favorable ventilation conditions were created by the explosion in order to ensure that the ensuing fire spread quickly. Such unusually good ventilation would not normally be present since the building is enclosed and the windows would be shut on a November evening. Lack of ventilation would be necessary for the explosion. That, in turn, would create the ventilation needed for the fire to spread. A professional would know how to blow out the windows. Another factor pointing to deliberate ignition is the rapid progress made by the fire. According to Ms. Smith, from 8:30 p.m., when she first discovered the fire, to 8:36 p.m., when the first fire trucks arrived at the scene, the fire had spread tremendously.

Field investigator and canine unit operator Henderson was present at the scene of the blaze, with his arson dog, Sparky. Sparky is trained to detect accelerants and other arson-related chemicals. Exhibits 13A and 13B are the scene photographs of Investigator Henderson and Sparky at the scene of the Flinders fire. Investigator Henderson reported that the fire had spread horizontally, which is another indication that good ventilation existed. Fire sweeps upward until it is blocked by some obstruction. When the fire is blocked, it travels through any available crack or opening. If there are no openings, the flames spread horizontally until the fire can sweep around the obstruction. When good ventilation conditions do not exist, the horizontal spread is slow. The fact that the horizontal travel of the fire was rapid indicates that favorable ventilation existed.

George Avery, whose body was found in the debris of the machine shop, died of multiple injuries resulting from the explosions. The autopsy report indicates that the fatal injury was to the chest. Field Investigator Henderson also obtained photographs of Avery's body at the scene, as well as photographs of the location of the body marked by outline tape the following morning. FI Henderson also took a photograph of the plant debris and remaining wall section after the fire was extinguished. The arson dog Sparky alerted to Avery's collar and also to an area on the floor just under Avery's collar. We took samples from the collar and floor for further forensic examination. It was later determined that the spots on the collar and floor were shampoo.

We had previously come into contact with Avery in connection with other investigations. Our normal practice in an arson case is to investigate all persons connected with the enterprise and, without exception, an investigation of any corpse found on the premises would be made.

Our investigation of Avery showed that he had been linked to two other fires that were of incendiary origin. One fire destroyed a factory owned by the Yaphank Co. Mr. Avery had been employed by Yaphank for only two weeks prior to the fire. The other fire destroyed a warehouse at the Fass Meatpacking Co. Although these fires were likely the result of arson, there was insufficient evidence for an arrest. Mr. Avery, who was associated with these businesses when the fires occurred, was questioned on both occasions. This marshal conducted both investigations. In connection with this investigation, I reviewed Avery's résumé, which I obtained from John Anderson at First Trust Bank. I checked with Cornell and MIT, schools Avery indicated on his résumé he had graduated from. Neither had any record of George Avery.

Contrary to popular belief, a substantial number of arsonists are trapped and killed in their own fires. For the most part, these persons are less than skilled at the techniques of arson. It is less likely that a professional arsonist would be caught in his own fire, but not particularly unusual.

CONCLUSION:

This marshal concludes that the fire was the result of arson. This conclusion is based upon the following factors:

1. The unusually large amount of hydrochloric acid that was located at the point of origin of the fire and apparently splashed about the room. Hydrogen likely was released and, in combination with ferrous metal, exploded by some sort of time release device that malfunctioned.

2. The unusually rapid spread of the fire, caused by favorable ventilation conditions not normally present.

3. The presence of George Avery in the building at the time of the fire.

Submitted by:

D Olsen

Donna Olsen, Chief

Form BFI 207

Olsen Memorandum

TO: File

FROM: Chief Olsen

DATE: January 3, YR-0

RE: Flinders Company Fire, 11/16/YR-1

I interviewed Arthur Jackson, president of Flinders Aluminum Fabrication Corp., at his home on January 3, YR-0. Jackson denied the arson. He admitted that Peterson had introduced him to Avery, the alleged designer. He seemed surprised (he said) by my assertion that Avery was a torch. I told him of Avery's work at the Yaphank Co. and that the Yaphank plant had burned down. He identified Avery as the man he hired to do design work, but denied knowledge of any fire at Yaphank. He reacted the same way when I told him of Avery's connection with the Fass Co., which also suffered a terrible fire.

He admitted paying Avery $50,000.

He admitted that HCl was kept at the plant in quantities of about fifty gallons.

I asked him if he personally checked on Avery's credentials listed on his résumé or any references Avery may have supplied. He said he left such matters to Ms. Peterson.

He said he had no motive because his wife had assets of around $1 million and he had personal assets of about $150,000.

On the evening of the fire, he visited the plant to pick up some papers from his office. This was at about 7 p.m. He left the plant by 7:30 p.m.

He said he dismissed Marie Williams from her position because she was becoming a pest and an embarrassment. He admitted that they had been lovers and asked if this information could be kept confidential.

Exhibit 6

Olsen Résumé

RÉSUMÉ OF DONNA OLSEN

EDUCATIONAL BACKGROUND:

Graduated from Darrow High School in Nita City in YR-34. Attended classes at Lincoln Community College in general curriculum from YR-34 to YR-32. Enlisted in United States Army in YR-32 and served in Fort Sill, Oklahoma, and Weisenstadt, Germany APO until YR-27.

Attended Nita Fire Department Training School in East Meadow, Nita, in YR-26, including basic courses in fire investigation and firefighting.

Completed an additional six-month arson investigation course at Nita Fire Department Training School and received certification by state and national training review agencies.

WORK HISTORY:

YR-25 to YR-20	Firefighter, East Meadow Fire Department, East Meadow, Nita; arson investigator for two years
YR-20 to YR-10	Marshal, Arson Bureau, East Meadow Fire Department, Nita
YR-10 to YR-5	Chief, Arson Bureau, East Meadow Fire Department, Nita
YR-5 to present	Chief, Nita Fire Department Bureau of Fire Investigation

FLINDERS FLOOR PLAN (FIRST FLOOR)

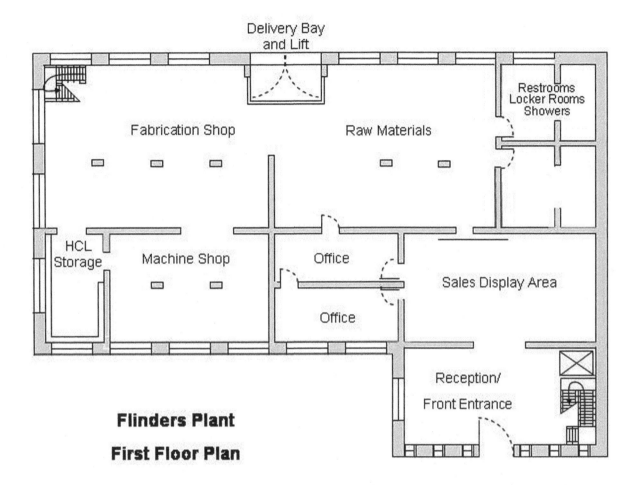

FLINDERS FLOOR PLAN (SECOND FLOOR)

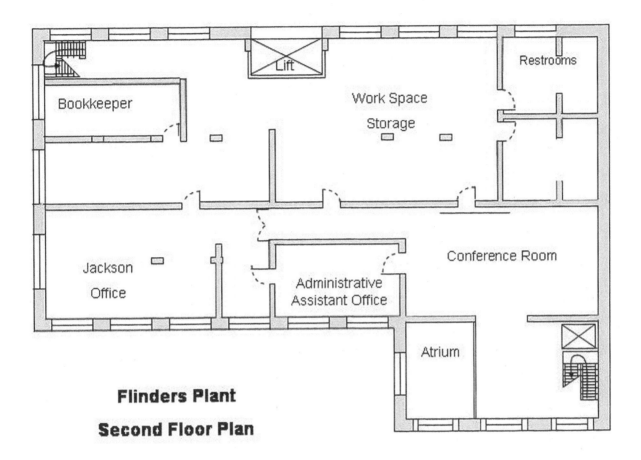

FLINDERS FLOOR PLAN (THIRD FLOOR)

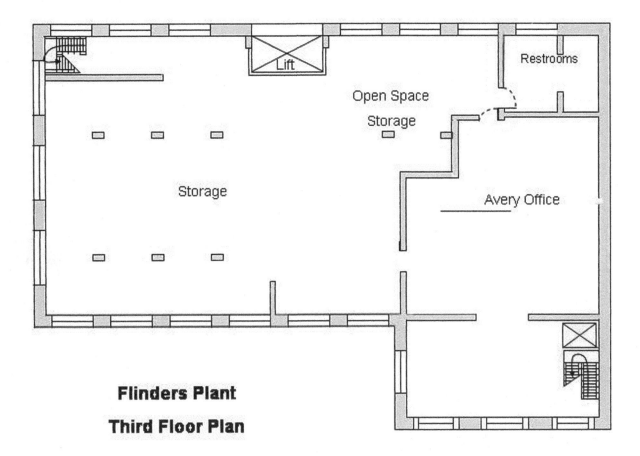

Exhibit 10

FLINDERS FLOOR PLAN (FOURTH FLOOR)

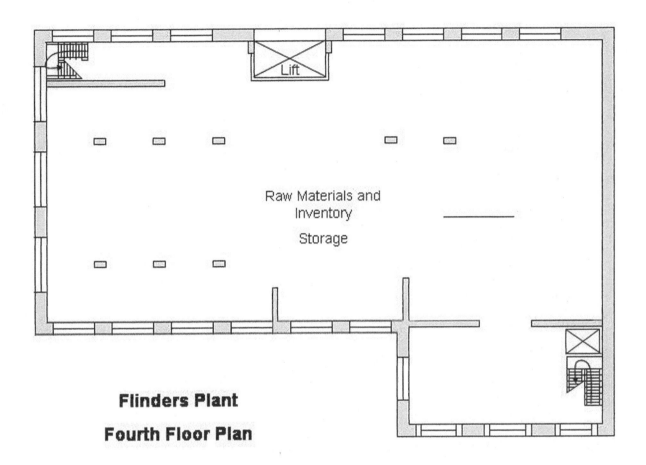

Raw Materials and
Inventory

Storage

Flinders Plant

Fourth Floor Plan

Exhibit 11

PHOTOGRAPH OF FLINDERS PRE-FIRE

Exhibit 12

PHOTOGRAPH OF FLINDERS POST-FIRE

Exhibit 13A

PHOTOGRAPH OF ARSON DOG SPARKY AT THE SCENE OF THE FLINDERS FIRE

Exhibit 13B

PHOTOGRAPH OF ARSON DOG SPARKY AT THE SCENE OF THE FLINDERS FIRE

PHOTOGRAPH OF FASS MEATPACKING CO.

PHOTOGRAPH OF YAPHANK CO.

2318 Crescent Street, Nita City
Phone (819) 555-6845
Email avery@nitamail.nita

George A. Avery

Education

YR-39 to YR-35	Cornell University, Bachelor of Science in Engineering Graduated *cum laude*
YR-35	Science Prize from University Board of Trustees
YR-35 to YR-33	Massachusetts Institute of Technology, Master of Arts Industrial Engineering Master's Thesis: "Metallurgical Processes in Industrial Grade Steel Fastener Failures"

Professional experience

YR-1	Fass Meatpacking Company, Tool and Die Design Consultant
YR-2	Yaphank Company, Metal Fittings Design
YR-4 to YR-3	Jefferson Aeronautics, Inc. Tool and Die Design
YR-6 to YR-5	Macauley Equipment Manufacturing, Tool and Die Design
YR-8 to YR-7	Ford Motor Company, Parts Integration
YR-10 to YR-9	General Dynamics, Engine Parts Testing and Design
YR-12 to YR-11	Ford Motor Company, Parts Integration
YR-15 to YR-13	McDonnell Douglas, Design Protocol Division
YR-16 to YR-15	McDonnell Douglas, Engine Tool and Die Unit
YR-18 to YR-17	General Dynamics, Senior Draftsman
YR-20 to YR-19	BMI, Senior Draftsman
YR-22 to YR-21	American Motors, Senior Draftsman
YR-26 to YR-23	Ross Metal Industries, Design Protocol
YR-28 to YR-26	Ross Metal Industries, Senior Draftsman
YR-30 to YR-29	Crown Engineering, Journeyman Draftsman
YR-33 to YR-30	Crown Engineering, Intern, Draftsman

Patents and publications

YR-16	Patent Application for Manifest Coupler U.S. Patent No. A78-3847659328

References

Suzanne Barker, American Motors, (760) 474-7285
Henry Arnett, Ross Metal Industries, (630) 243-0956
Jack Darnell, General Dynamics Corporation, (890) 583-3487

GEORGE AVERY PHOTOGRAPH

Exhibit 18

PHOTOGRAPH OF AVERY BODY OUTLINE

Exhibit 19

AVERY CHECK

Flinders Aluminum Fabricating Corp.
187 River Road
Nita City, Nita 99990

13628
71-74242712

Date **September 15, YR-1**

Pay to
the Order of   George Avery $ 50,000.00

Ten Thousand & 00/100   Dollars

FIRST TRUST BANK
Nita City, Nita 99990
271274241: 13 628 000500000

Marie Williams

Exhibit 20

AUTOPSY REPORT

STATE OF NITA
COUNTY OF DARROW

Office of Medical Examiner
(721) 555-3200

County/City Building
Nita City, Nita 57817

AUTOPSY REPORT
George Avery

Information available at time of autopsy:

This fifty-seven-year-old Caucasian male was found beneath the debris of an explosion at a local aluminum plant.

Under the provisions of Nita Code 21-205, a postmortem examination including autopsy of the body is performed in the Darrow County Medical Examiner's Office on November 17, YR-1, commencing at 10:00 a.m.

External examination of the body:

The decedent is brought to the morgue in a disaster bag. Clothing includes a blue plaid, long-sleeved shirt on which the sleeves are burned and the seams on the sleeves are torn, a pair of blue jeans that have numerous types of particulate debris on them, a pair of white briefs, a pair of white crew socks, and a pair of white Nike tennis shoes. These items of clothing are forwarded to the Crime Laboratory.

This is the unembalmed body of a white male weighing 175 pounds and measuring six feet in height. The stature is mesomorphic, rigor mortis is generalized, and lividity is dorsal and not fixed and has a pinkish discoloration. No other decompositional changes are noted, and the overall appearance of the body is that of a well-developed white male, consistent with the stated age of fifty-seven years. The hair is light brown, of medium length, and shows frontal parietal balding. Portions of the hair in the frontal region have been scorched. The external auditory meati are unremarkable. The irises are blue and the pupils are equally dilated. The nasal and oral cavities contain a small amount of bloody froth. The teeth are the decedent's natural teeth and are in average condition. There are first- and second-degree burns over the skin of the face and cheeks and there is a 3.5 cm angulated laceration over the ramus of the right mandible, which is a full thickness laceration and appears to represent some impact with an object which has a right angle on its surface.

The neck is unremarkable.

The upper extremities are remarkable in that there are first- and second-degree burns over the skin of the hands and distal forearms, and there is a compound fracture of the right humerus.

The torso is remarkable in that there are numerous fractures of the ribs bilaterally that can be palpated through the skin. There are three small ecchymoses over the left pectoral region, and there are numerous superficial scrapes over the skin of the lumbar region. On the back, there is a three-inch in diameter circular contusion that is definitely patterned and is essentially a series of 1 cm arcs that form a "broken circle." It is located over the right scapula.

The external genitalia are those of a normal adult male, the penis is circumcised, and both testes are descended.

The lower extremities are remarkable only in that there are several ecchymoses over the anterior surfaces of both tibias that are of various ages, and there are several acute contusions over the right patella.

Internal examination of the body:

Head

The skin of the scalp is retracted in the usual manner, and there are several areas of soft tissue hemorrhage in the scalp over the right and left frontal parietal regions.

The underlying calvarium is intact, and upon its removal there is no blood in the epidural, subdural, or subarachnoid space. The cerebral gyri are moderately broadened and flattened, and the sulci are moderately obliterated. Coronal sectioning of the 1250 gram brain demonstrates no gross abnormalities other than cerebral edema. There is no herniation. The dura is reflected from the base of the skull, and there is no evidence of basilar skull trauma.

Chest and Abdomen

The skin of the chest and abdomen is opened with the usual Y-shaped incision, which demonstrates a 1 cm layer of yellow subcutaneous adipose tissue. There is moderate amount of hemorrhage in the subcutaneous fat over the chest and abdomen. Upon reflection of the skin flaps, the right ribs two through six can be palpated to be fractured in the axillary line, and the left ribs two through seven have been fractured in the anterior axillary line.

Upon removal of the chest plate, there is a bilateral hemothorax totaling two liters. The rib fractures have penetrated the parietal pleura and have caused bilateral pulmonary contusions and lacerations. Both lungs are collapsed.

The skin of the neck is dissected up to the angle of the jaw and there is no evidence of soft tissue trauma to the major airways or vital surrounding structure of the lateral neck compartments.

The thoracic and abdominal organs are examined in situ, then removed by the Virchow technique for serial examination.

Major Airways

The larynx, trachea, and major bronchi are unremarkable except that there is a small amount of blood adherent to the mucosa, and there is a moderate amount of soot in the airways.

Lungs

The right lung weighs 500 grams, and the left lung 460 grams. Both lungs are collapsed and atelectatic. There are bilateral pulmonary contusions, and there is mild anthracotic change on the pleural surfaces. There are no mass lesions seen on serial sectioning of the lungs. There are focal areas of parenchymal hemorrhage surrounding the pulmonary contusions, and the pulmonary veins have been lacerated bilaterally at the hila.

Heart

The heart weighs 290 grams. There is concentric left ventricle hypertrophy. The epicardium, endocardium, valve leaflets, and chordae tendineae are unremarkable. The coronary arteries show mild atherosclerotic plaquing, but the degree of occlusion is not significant.

Gastrointestinal Tract

The esophagus is unremarkable. The stomach contains two cups of partially digested food, which consists primarily of noodles with a small amount of slightly chewed meat which appears to be beef. The small bowel, large bowel, appendix, and rectum are unremarkable.

Hepatobiliary System

The liver weighs 1900 grams and is congested. The gall bladder contains 15 ml of watery green bile and no stones. The extra hepatic biliary ducts are patent.

Spleen

The spleen weighs 120 grams, has a wrinkled capsule, and has a small laceration near the posterior pole of the hilum. There is about 150 ml of blood in the splenic bed.

Pancreas

The pancreas weighs 110 grams, has a coarsely lobulated appearance, and soft consistency on cross section.

Urinary System

The right kidney weighs 140 grams, and the left kidney 150 grams. Both capsules strip easily from the cortical surfaces, and the kidneys have the typical cortex and dark medulla consistent with "shock kidney." The ureters are unremarkable, and the bladder mucosa is within normal limits. The bladder contains about 150 ml of dilute urine.

Endocrines

The thyroid and adrenals are unremarkable. The parathyroids are not identified.

Great Vessels

The great vessels of the thorax and abdomen and the tributaries thereof are unremarkable except for acute trauma to the pulmonary veins noted above.

Other procedures:

1) Blood and urine are submitted for toxicology.

2) Documentary photographs are taken.

3) Clothing is submitted to the Crime Laboratory for accelerant analysis.

4) Autopsy diagrams marked with location of injuries.

Gross diagnoses:

1) First- and second-degree burns to face and distal forearms and hands.

2) Bilateral rib fractures and bilateral pneumothorax and hemothorax.

3) Bilateral pulmonary contusions with lacerations of pulmonary vein.

4) Compound fracture of right humerus.

5) Laceration of spleen.

6) Patterned contusion, back.

7) Patterned laceration, skin over right mandible.

Causes of death:

BLUNT TRAUMA, PRIMARILY TO CHEST causing victim to hemorrhage into chest cavity. Combination of trauma from blow and blood in chest cavity resulted in collapse of lungs and inability to breathe.

Ronald Harrison
Ronald Harrison, MD
Medical Examiner
RH:sd

Date: November 18, YR-1

Exhibit 21

AUTOPSY DIAGRAM (FRONT TO REAR)

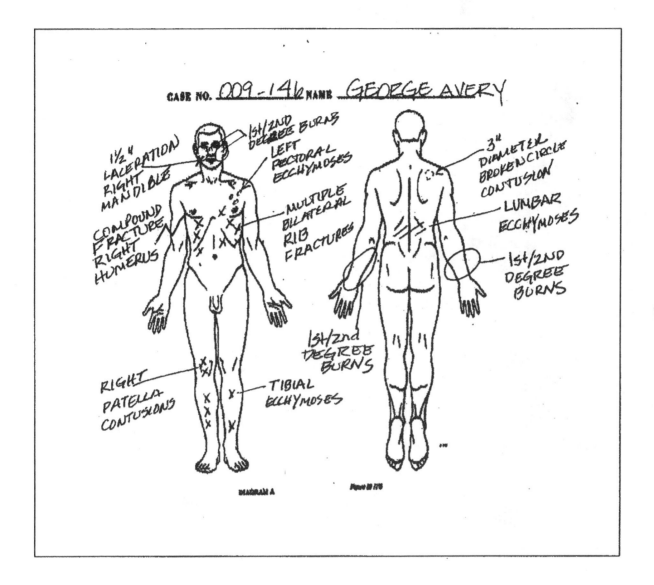

AUTOPSY DIAGRAM (HAND)

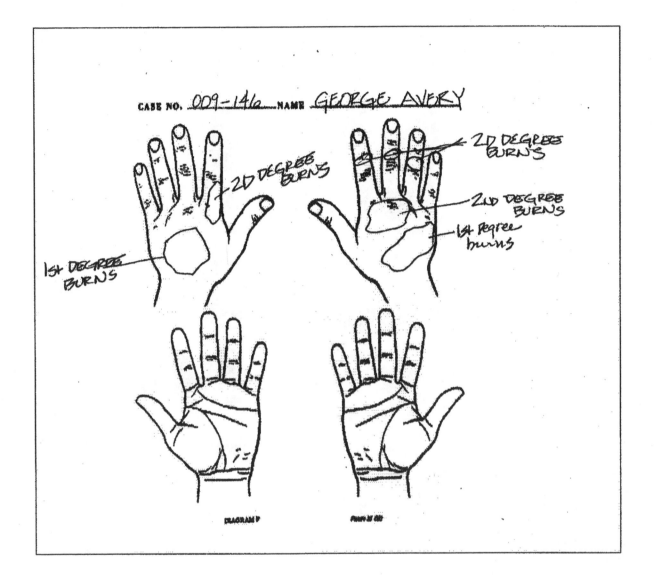

AUTOPSY DIAGRAM (SIDE)

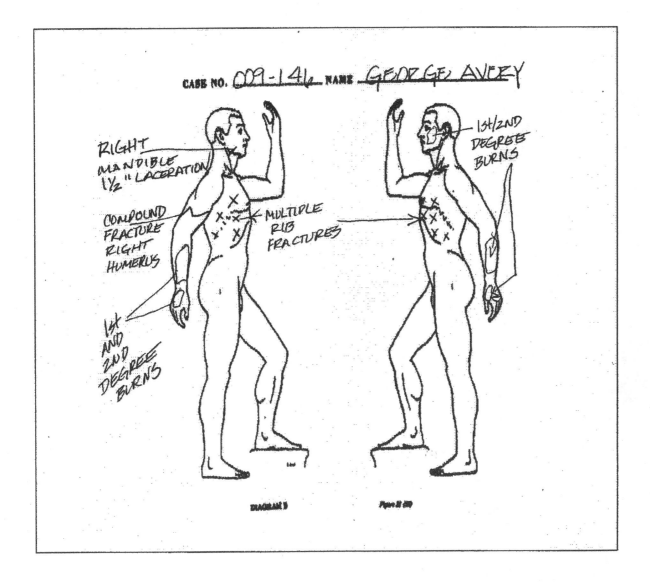

Exhibit 24

ACCELERANT ANALYSIS REPORT

CITY OF NITA POLICE DEPARTMENT

CRIME LABORATORY

ACCELERANT ANALYSIS REPORT

Physical Evidence Section	Agency:	Bureau of Fire
232 Barnett	File: Investigator:	6374
Nita City, Nita	Charge: Report Date: Examination by:	Olsen NC 20-305
Subject: Flinders Aluminum Fabrication Corp.		December 1, YR-1 Victoria Faris, Senior Criminalist

At the request of Chief Fire Marshal Olsen, clothing samples were examined for the presence of hydrochloric acid, iron filings, and shampoo. The clothing samples were reportedly from the deceased, George Avery, and were forwarded to the Crime Laboratory by the Office of the Medical Examiner on November 17, YR-1. Returned to Olsen on December 1, YR-1.

Laboratory Examination

The following items were received:

   Item 1, a blue plaid shirt with burnt sleeves

   Item 2, blue jeans

   Item 3, white briefs

   Item 4, white crew socks

   Item 5, a pair of white Nike athletic shoes

The clothing items were visually examined for particles, for stains indicative of acid exposure, and for shampoo residue. Stains on the blue jeans were tested for acidity (pH) and examined with X-ray fluorescence spectrometry (XRF) and chemical spot tests. Particulate debris from the blue jeans was examined with X-ray fluorescence spectrometry (XRF). A solid residue from the plaid shirt collar was tested for surfactant (sudsing) properties. Aqueous extracts of the soles of the Nike shoes were tested for pH and examined with X-ray fluorescence spectrometry (XRF) and chemical spot tests. The lower parts of the sleeves of the shirt were burnt away and could not be examined for pH.

Examination Conclusions and Observations

No indications of hydrochloric acid, such as acidity or chloride, were found on the blue jeans or the soles of the Nike shoes. This does not mean the items were not exposed to hydrochloric acid under circumstances in which it did not survive on the clothing, such as dilution or exposure to heat. A variety of metallic particles were found on the blue jeans, including aluminum, iron, and some with a composition of iron, nickel, and chromium, which are found in stainless steel. The solid residue from the left shirt collar exhibited sudsing properties when mixed with water, as would be expected from shampoo or soap products. No other tests were performed on the solid residue. This laboratory cannot determine the brand of shampoo.

Exhibit 25

REPORT OF DAVID PINKUS

RE: Fire at Flinders Aluminum Fabrication Corporation's industrial plant, 187 River Road, Nita City

DATE OF FIRE: November 16, YR-1   **DATE OF REPORT:** May 1, YR-0

I have thoroughly reviewed the report of Chief Fire Marshal Olsen. My analysis of the facts in her report leads me to conclude that the fire must be technically listed as an accident. My review and analysis are conducted pursuant to pertinent provisions of the National Fire Protection Association Guide 921. In the course of my analysis, I reviewed all reports and memos from Chief Olsen; the three fire videos of the fires at Fass, Yaphank, and Flinders; the autopsy report performed on George Avery; photographs of the scene taken close to the time of the Flinders fire; and the accelerant analysis report provided by the Crime Laboratory.

Hydrochloric acid is normally present at the plant because it is used to clean the aluminum products. Since it is stored in one place, this would explain the large quantity of hydrochloric acid at the point or origin of the fire. Chief Olsen's conclusion that hundreds of gallons were splashed about the room is pure conjecture based not on physical evidence, but upon the size of the fire. The explosion itself could explain the searing of the concrete and the presence of HCl in the debris. Given the elapsed time between ignition and observation, no conclusion as to the amount of acid involved or whether it was spread about is possible.

The smoke and flame of the fire were not observed until the fire was burning for one-half hour. By this time, the building was being consumed by the fire. At this point, the color of the smoke and flame is affected by the burning building and not the acid.

In my opinion, the rapid spread of the fire could have been caused by several factors. First, from my previous visits to the plant during fire prevention duties, the rooms were large, with considerable fuel loading, open, and provided favorable ventilation conditions that would encourage the fire to spread. Although the remaining structure showed that a window was open, there is no way of knowing if the other windows were open or closed, because most of the structure was destroyed. Second, since the building was very old, it was not constructed to prevent fire travel, nor was it constructed to prevent many causes of accidental fires. Third, an accidental explosion involving fifty gallons of hydrochloric acid would result in the conflagration described in Chief Olsen's report. Fourth, accidental explosion would account for the fatality. It is unlikely that a professional arsonist would be so careless as to be caught in a fire of his own making.

Chief Olsen has not ruled out, nor could she, the possibility that a leak in a storage drum holding HCl could have resulted in the introduction of the acid throughout the storage room. If the acid came into contact with hot ferrous metal from any cause, an explosion could result.

The sheer magnitude of the physical destruction caused by the explosion, fire, and the volume of water poured on the fire would have washed away evidence of accidental causes such as faulty wiring, cigarette butts, and the like.

In arson investigations, no finding of arson should be made until all possible accidental causes are ruled out. Since accidental causes of the fire have not been satisfactorily eliminated, I am unable to conclude that the fire was the result of arson. As to the presence of Mr. Avery, I agree with Chief Olsen that his background should be gone into in some detail. Some of that background is disquieting. However, there is insufficient evidence to establish that Avery is an arsonist. Moreover, there is little evidence in this case, other than circumstances, to link him to the fire.

Submitted by:

David Pinkus
David Pinkus

Exhibit 26

Pɪɴᴋᴜꜱ Cᴜʀʀɪᴄᴜʟᴜᴍ Vɪᴛᴀᴇ

DAVID G. PINKUS
CURRICULUM VITAE

YR-5–Present **Consultant and Lecturer in Arson Investigation Techniques**
For past six years, have worked as a forensic consultant in both civil and criminal cases involving unexplained fires and explosions. Have worked for both plaintiffs and defendants in civil cases and both the state and the defendant in criminal cases. Have lectured at a number of seminars on the subject of modernizing arson investigation techniques.

YR-10–YR-5 **Chief Fire Marshal, Nita City Bureau of Fire Investigation**
Appointed Chief Fire Marshal in charge of arson investigation. Supervised an investigation team that grew from three investigators to twenty investigators. Attended a series of six national seminars on aspects of arson investigation, including uses of accelerants, explosives, household compounds, and commonly available chemicals and ignition devices.

Have taught courses in arson investigation and investigative procedures at the Nita City Bureau of Fire Investigation and at the Nita Fire Department Training School in East Meadow.

Retired from the Bureau with commendation, February 6, YR-5.

YR-28–YR-10 **Firefighter, Fire Investigator, Nita City Fire Department**
Attended Firefighter Training Academy, Nita City, followed by two years' service as a firefighter for the Fire Department. Involved in multiple firefighting operations, including residential and commercial structures and involving multiple mechanisms of fire initiation.

Joined the National Fire Emergency Rescue team and engaged in forest fire fighting operations in Yellowstone National Park, Colorado, and Idaho.

Accepted for intensive training in arson investigation offered by Colorado College, followed by two years' service as an arson investigator in the Nita City Bureau of Fire Investigation.

YR-33–YR-29	*United States Navy* *Officer Candidate School* *Service, Manila, Philippines; Guam*

While in service, assigned various combat and non-combat duties. Received specialized training in fighting on-ship fires, including aircraft carriers, destroyers, and patrols. Was assigned supervisory responsibility for on-board firefighting teams during wartime operations. Achieved rank of lieutenant.

PROFESSIONAL ASSOCIATIONS AND ORGANIZATIONS

Past president, Nita State Association of Firefighters

National Board Member, National Association of Firefighters

Member, Joint Task Force Nita City/County Arson Investigation Modernization

Member and Past Vice President, National Emergency Response Team

PUBLICATIONS

National Association of Firefighters Newsletter, "Short Fuse Ignition Devices in Intentionally Set Fires," Vol. 4: 28–32 (YR-12)

Chapter, "Modern Techniques for Site Recovery of Accelerant Residue," in *Arson Investigation*, Houghton Miflin (YR-5)

Exhibit 27

VIDEO OF FLINDERS FIRE (AVAILABLE VIA NITA'S DIGITAL DOWNLOAD CENTER)

http://bit.ly/1P20Jea
Password: Flinders11

Exhibit 28

Video of Yaphank Fire (Available via NITA's Digital Download Center)

http://bit.ly/1P20Jea
Password: Flinders11

Exhibit 29

VIDEO OF FASS FIRE (AVAILABLE VIA NITA'S DIGITAL DOWNLOAD CENTER)

http://bit.ly/1P20Jea
Password: Flinders11

Exhibit 30

ANDERSON BANK MEMO

First Trust Bank
Nita City, Nita 12305

MEMORANDUM

TO: Gerald Laughlin

           Loan Review Committee

FROM: John Anderson, Vice President

DATE: October 15, YR-1

RE: Flinders Transition Plan

I have had several meetings this month with Arthur Jackson, president of Flinders Aluminum, in which he has requested new financing and an adjustment of current financing with the bank. I have reviewed the proposed concept of transitioning the Flinders Aluminum plant that currently manufactures siding for housing to an auto parts manufacturing plant and am seeking additional information from our client in this regard. Given the admitted recent earnings track record at Flinders, the time has come for such a transition and, if handled deftly, this could be a very promising investment. I have asked the client to provide financial data, market studies, tax returns, and product designs (surprisingly, none have been provided to date), which, if they pan out, will encourage our participation. The land value alone in this riverfront area could provide the requisite security for any investment.

I will advise when the follow-up information arrives.

EMAIL FROM ARTHUR JACKSON TO JANICE JACKSON

Arthur Jackson

From:	Arthur Jackson <arthur@flindersalum.nita>
Sent:	Wednesday, October 5, YR-1 9:23 a.m.
To:	Janice Jackson (jj@nitalink.nita)
Subject:	A favor

Hi Janice:

I am really sorry that you and I are not talking.

As you know, business at the plant has been very slow since last year and we are having a hard time making ends meet. On top of that, we have a large loan with our bank that is due next month and I'm not sure we have enough cash on hand to make the payment. I have come up with a business plan that I believe will bring the company back, but in the meantime I need additional resources to bring this plan to fruition and work out my finances with the bank, so I'm hoping that you can loan me $100,000 out of your inheritance investments to tide me over until I turn things around.

Many thanks in advance,
Art

Arthur Jackson President
Flinders Aluminum Fabrication Corporation
187 River Road
Nita City, Nita 57816
(819) 555-5000
arthur@flindersalum.nita

Exhibit 32

Janice Jackson

From:	Janice Jackson <jj@nitalink.nita>
Sent:	Thursday, October 6, YR-1 10:45 a.m.
To:	Art Jackson
Subject:	Not a chance!

I can't believe you think I would take money out of the account I am keeping for our children and their future to help you try to pull off some cockamamie plan to rescue your failing business. Use your own damn money or, absent that, ask your new girlfriend, Sonia, for the money.

Janice Jackson
1200 East Gate
Nita City, Nita 57820
jj@nitalink.nita

From:	Arthur Jackson <arthur@flindersalum.nita>
Sent:	Wednesday, October 5, YR-1 9:23 a.m.
To:	Janice Jackson (jj@nitalink.nita)
Subject:	A favor

Hi Janice:

I am really sorry that you and I are not talking.

As you know, business at the plant has been very slow since last year and we are having a hard time making ends meet. On top of that, we have a large loan with our bank that is due next month and I'm not sure we have enough cash on hand to make the payment. I have come up with a business plan that I believe will bring the company back, but in the meantime I need additional resources to bring this plan to fruition and work out my finances with the bank, so I'm hoping that you can loan me $100,000 out of your inheritance investments to tide me over until I turn things around.

Many thanks in advance,

Art
Arthur Jackson President
Flinders Aluminum Fabrication Corporation
187 River Road
Nita City, Nita 57816
(819) 555-5000
arthur@flindersalum.nita

Exhibit 33

EMAILS BETWEEN SONIA PETERSON AND ARTHUR JACKSON

Arthur Jackson

From:	Arthur Jackson <arthur@flindersalum.nita>
Sent:	Thursday, July 11, YR-1 8:15 a.m.
To:	Sonia Peterson (sonia@nitamail.nita)
Subject:	Re: Introduction

Thank you, Ms. Peterson, for your interest in my company. You have an interesting background. I'm particularly impressed with your work at Yaphank and would like to hear more about it. Would you have time to meet with me at the plant sometime early next week? You can also text me for further details if you wish.

Arthur
Arthur Jackson
President
Flinders Aluminum Fabrication Corporation
187 River Road
Nita City, Nita 57816
(819) 555-5000
arthur@flindersalum.nita

From:	Sonia Peterson <sonia@nitamail.nita>
Sent:	Wednesday, July 10, YR-1 2:13 p.m.
To:	Arthur Jackson (arthur@flindersalum.nita)
Subject:	Introduction
Attachment:	SPeterson_Resume.docx

Dear Mr. Jackson:

I believe we should meet. I have an extensive background in strategic planning, marketing, product development, and obtaining venture capital for startups and businesses in need of capital infusion. Word on the street is that Flinders is going through hard times and needs a turn-around strategy, which is right up my alley. And the timing couldn't be better, since I'm looking for a new challenge where I can get in on the ground floor of a solid, industrially based company.

My résumé is attached for your review. If you are interested, please call me at 819-555-0828 to set up an appointment.

Sonia Peterson

Exhibit 34

RÉSUMÉ OF SONIA PETERSON

SONIA PETERSON
88 CHARING CROSS MUSE
NITA CITY, NITA
819-555-0828
SONIA@NITAMAIL.NITA

Career Profile

Experienced Marketing Consultant and Administrative Assistant with excellent organizational skills and emphasis on developing new businesses and product lines.

Skills and Proficiencies

- All standard word processing programs, including Word, Excel, and accounting and presentation software
- Marketing research and pro forma statements for business development and new product lines
- Customer service programming
- Business planning on monthly, quarterly, and annual basis
- Financial and credit research and presentations
- Employee benefit programs and human resource organization
- Purchasing and invoicing

Employment History

June YR-12–May YR-8   Firehouse Insurance Company

Entry-level position in commercial department. Responsible for transcription, customer contacts, correspondence, document review, and proofing. Was promoted after six months to assistant administrative supervisor of secretarial pool. After two years was promoted to administrative supervisor of the secretarial pool, with responsibilities for interfacing with management and establishing employee workforce and development planning.

June YR-8–June YR-2   Yaphank Company

Administrative supervisor of development of new product lines including commercial and industrial storm shutters and accompanying business plans for submission to lenders and potential customers. Responsible for market research, market development, customer contacts, and strategic long-term planning. Oversaw product line development from market entry stage to significant expansion of market share in sales of commercial and industrial shutters and window protection systems.

July YR-2–present   Peterson, Miltown & Associates

Partner in venture capital enterprise concentrating on start-up companies in the field of manufacturing. Client list includes several companies that have established success in manufacturing a variety of products, including automobile parts, brick veneer construction systems, commercial security devices, and cold weather paint application systems.

Education

YR-12   Nita State University

BA in Business, emphasis on marketing and development of new businesses. Graduated *magna cum laude*. Received Chamber of Commerce Award for "Ideas in Business Innovation," Spring Semester YR-12.

TEXT MESSAGES BETWEEN SONIA PETERSON AND ARTHUR JACKSON

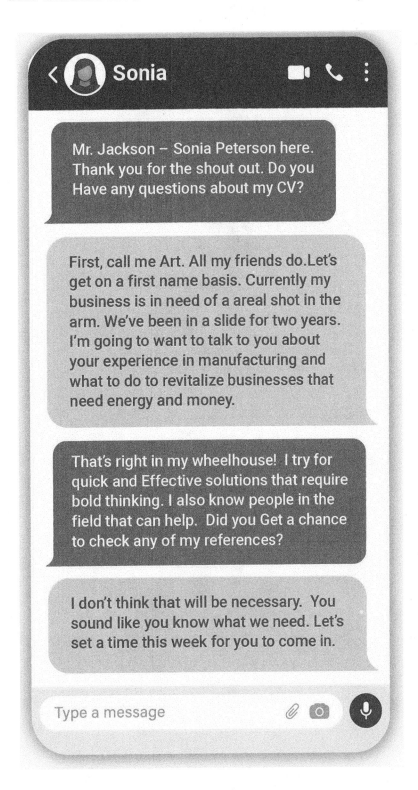

Exhibit 36

Text Messages between Sonia Peterson and George Avery

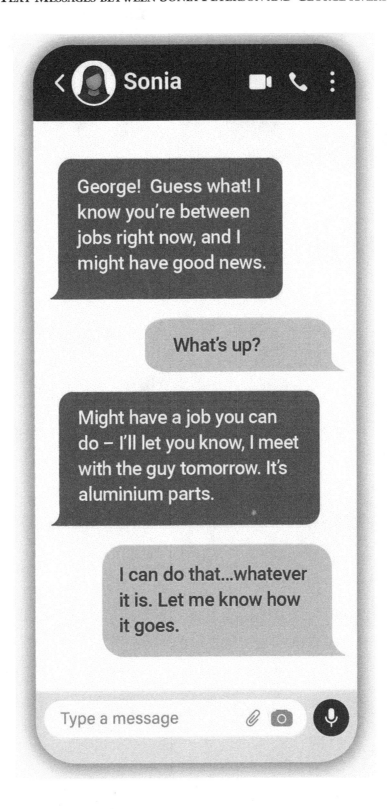

Exhibit 37

EMAILS BETWEEN MATTHEW KORN AND JACK DARNELL

Korn, Matthew

From:	Jack Darnell [jack.darnell@generaldynamics.nita]
Sent:	June 10, YR-2 1:18 p.m.
To:	Korn, Matthew [mkorn@yaphankco.nita]
Subject:	Re: George A. Avery

Matt: To tell you the truth, I do not remember him well. He worked alone and did not socialize either during work or after with anyone. He was only there in my division for a short while, maybe three or four months before he left. His work for us was fine. I wish I had more info.

See you July 4 at the Club?
Jack
Jack Darnell
Division Chief
General Dynamics Corporation
1256 Alamo Parkway
East Meadow, Nita

From:	Korn, Matthew [mkorn@yaphankco.nita]
Sent:	June 10, YR-2 11:09 a.m.
To:	Jack Darnell [jack.darnell@generaldynamics.nita]
Subject:	George A. Avery

Jack: I hope this email finds you well. I am checking out George A. Avery, an engineer who I am thinking of hiring to assist with a tool and die design position. He has listed you as a reference and shows his employment at General Dynamics as a Senior Draftsman in YR-18 to YR-17 and working in Engine Parts Testing and Design in YR-10 to YR-9. What can you tell me about him?

Matt
Matthew Korn
President
Yaphank Company
1551 Green Street
Nita City, Nita

Exhibit 38

PINKUS MEMORANDUM

MEMORANDUM

TO: Counsel for Mismo Fire Insurance
FROM: Legal Assistant
RE: David Pinkus

At your request, I have checked with several attorneys about plaintiff's fire expert in the Flinders case, David Pinkus.

Mr. Pinkus is known more by criminal attorneys for his opinions in alleged arson cases. He is thought of as fair-minded and balanced in his approach. Both the prosecution and defense have retained him in such cases, as stated in his résumé. In the civil arena, Mr. Pinkus has been retained primarily (somewhere in the neighborhood of 90 percent of the time, from what I can tell) by members of the plaintiff's bar to refute charges of arson leveled by insurance companies when denying damage claims due to fire. Nobody I talked to remembers him ever testifying in civil court that a fire was purposefully set. Rather, he usually attacks the findings of the investigation team.

Based on counsel's 26(a)(2)(B) disclosure, he is paid $300 an hour for consulting work and report writing, $3,000 a day (and $2,000 for half a day) when testifying at deposition or in court, and has thus far billed $3,000 in this case for phone calls, meetings, review of material, and writing his report.

Exhibit 39

EXCERPT FROM NFPA GUIDE 921*

Chapter 4. Basic Methodology

4.1 Nature of Fire Investigations. A fire or explosion investigation is a complex endeavor involving skill, technology, knowledge, and science. The compilation of factual data, as well as an analysis of those facts, should be accomplished objectively, truthfully, and without expectation, bias, preconception, or prejudice. The basic methodology of the fire investigation should rely on the use of a systematic approach and attention to all relevant details. The use of a systematic approach often will uncover new factual data for analysis, which may require previous conclusions to be reevaluated. With few exceptions, the proper methodology for a fire or explosion investigation is to first determine and establish the origin(s), then investigate the cause: circumstances, conditions, or agencies that brought the ignition source, fuel, and oxidant together.

4.2 Systematic Approach. The systematic approach recommended is that of the scientific method, which is used in the physical sciences (*see Figure 4.3*).

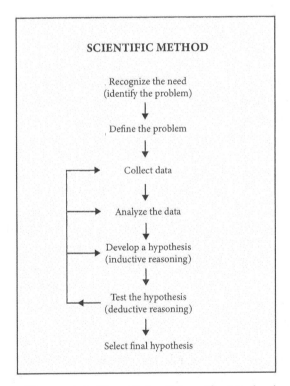

Figure 4.3: Use of the Scientific Method.

4.3.2 Define the Problem. Having determined that a problem exists, the investigator or analyst should define the manner in which the problem can be solved. In this case, a proper origin and cause investigation should be conducted. This is done by an examination of the scene and by a combination of other data collection methods, such as the review of previously conducted investigations of the incident, the interviewing of witnesses or other knowledgeable persons, and the results of scientific testing.

4.3.3 Collect Data. Facts about the fire incident are now collected by observation, experiment, or other direct data gathering means. The data collected is called empirical data because it is based on observation or experience and is capable of being verified or known to be true.

4.3.4 Analyze the Data. The scientific method requires that all data collected be analyzed. This is an essential step that must take place before the formation of the final hypothesis. The identification, gathering, and cataloging of data does not equate to data analysis. Analysis of the data is based on the knowledge, training, experience, and expertise of the individual doing the analysis. If the investigator lacks expertise to properly attribute meaning to a piece of data, then assistance should be sought. Understanding the meaning of the data will enable the investigator to form hypotheses based on the evidence, rather than on speculation.

4.3.5 Develop a Hypothesis (Inductive Reasoning). Based on the data analysis, the investigator produces a hypothesis, or hypotheses, to explain the phenomena, whether it be the nature of fire patterns, fire spread, identification of the origin, the ignition sequence, the fire cause, or the causes of damage or responsibility for the fire or explosion incident. This process is referred to as inductive reasoning. These hypotheses should be based solely on the empirical data that the investigator has collected through observation and then developed into explanations for the event, which are based upon the investigator's knowledge, training, experience, and expertise.

4.3.6 Test the Hypothesis (Deductive Reasoning). The investigator does not have a valid hypothesis unless it can stand the test of careful and serious challenge. Testing of the hypothesis is done by the principle of deductive reasoning, in which the investigator compares his or her hypothesis to all the known facts as well as the body of scientific knowledge associated with the phenomena relevant to the specific incident. A hypothesis can be tested either physically by conducting experiments or analytically by applying scientific principles in "thought experiments." When relying on experiments or research of others, the investigator must ensure that the conditions and circumstances are sufficiently similar. When the investigator relies on previously conducted research, references to the research relied upon should be noted. If the hypothesis cannot be supported, it should be discarded and alternate hypotheses should be developed and tested. This may include the collection of new data or the reanalysis of existing data. The testing process needs to be continued until all feasible hypotheses have been tested and one is determined to be uniquely consistent with the facts, and with the principles of science. If no hypothesis can withstand an examination by deductive reasoning, the issue should be considered undetermined.

4.3.6.1 Any hypothesis that is incapable of being tested is an invalid hypothesis. A hypothesis developed based on the absence of data is an example of a hypothesis that is incapable of being tested. The inability to refute a hypothesis does not mean that the hypothesis is true.

4.3.7 Avoid Presumption. Until data have been collected, no specific hypothesis can be reasonably formed or tested. All investigations of fire and explosion incidents should be approached by the investigator without presumption as to origin, ignition sequence, cause, fire spread, or responsibility for the incident until the use of scientific method has yielded testable hypotheses, which cannot be disproved by rigorous testing.

4.3.8 Expectation Bias. Expectation bias is a well-established phenomenon that occurs in scientific analysis when investigator(s) reach a premature conclusion without having examined or considered all of the relevant data. Instead of collecting and examining all of the data in a logical and unbiased manner to reach a scientifically reliable conclusion, the investigator(s) uses the premature determination to dictate investigative processes, analyses, and, ultimately, conclusions, in a way that is not scientifically valid. The introduction of expectation bias into the investigation results in the use of only that data that supports this previously formed conclusion and often results in the misinterpretation and/or the discarding of data that does not support the original opinion. Investigators are strongly cautioned to avoid expectation bias through proper use of the scientific method.

4.3.9 Confirmation Bias. Different hypotheses may be compatible with the same data. When using the scientific method, testing of hypotheses should be designed to disprove the hypothesis. Confirmation bias occurs when the investigator instead tries to prove the hypothesis. This can result in failure to consider alternate hypotheses. A hypothesis can be said to be valid only when rigorous testing has failed to disprove the hypothesis.

4.4.3 Conducting the Investigation.

4.4.3.1 It is during this stage of the investigation that an examination of the incident fire or explosion scene is conducted. The fundamental purpose of conducting an examination of any incident scene is to collect all of the available data and document the incident scene. The investigator should conduct an examination of the scene if it is available and collect data necessary to the analysis.

4.4.3.2 The actual investigation may include different steps and procedures, which will be determined by the purpose of the assignment. These steps and procedures are described in detail elsewhere in the document. A fire or explosion investigation may include all or some of the following tasks: a scene inspection or review of previous scene documentation done by others; scene documentation through photography and diagramming; evidence recognition, documentation, and preservation; witness interviews; review and analysis of the investigations of others; and identification and collection of data from other appropriate sources.

4.4.5 Analyzing the Incident. All collected and available data should be analyzed using the principles of the scientific method. Depending on the nature and scope of one's assignment, hypotheses should be developed and tested explaining the origin, ignition sequence, fire spread, fire cause or causes of damage or casualties, or responsibility for the incident.

4.4.6 Conclusions. Conclusions, which are final hypotheses, are drawn as a result of testing the hypotheses. Conclusions should be drawn according to the principles expressed in this guide and reported appropriately.

4.5 Level of Certainty. The level of certainty describes how strongly someone holds an opinion (conclusion). Someone may hold any opinion to a higher or lower level of certainty. That level is determined by assessing the investigator's confidence in the data, in the analysis of that data, and testing of hypotheses formed. That level of certainty may determine the practical application of the opinion, especially in legal proceedings.

Chapter 18. Determining the Cause

18.6.5 Inappropriate Use of the Process of Elimination. The process of determining the ignition source for a fire, by eliminating all ignition sources found, known, or believed to have been present in the area of origin, and then claiming such methodology is proof of an ignition source for which there is no evidence of existence, is referred to by some investigators as "negative corpus." Negative corpus has typically been used in classifying fires as incendiary, although the process has also been used to characterize fires classified as accidental. This process is not consistent with the Scientific Method, is inappropriate, and should not be used because it generates un-testable hypotheses and may result in incorrect determinations of the ignition source and first fuel ignited. Any hypothesis formulated for the causal factors (e.g., first fuel, ignition source, and ignition sequence) must be based on facts. Those facts are derived from evidence, observations, calculations, experiments, and the laws of science. Speculative information cannot be included in the analysis.

> **18.6.5.1 Cause Undetermined.** In the circumstance where all hypothesized fire causes have been eliminated and the investigator is left with no hypothesis that is evidenced by the facts of the investigation, the only choice for the investigator is to opine that the fire cause, or specific causal factors, remains undetermined. It is improper to base hypotheses on the absence of any supportive evidence (see 11.5.2, Types of Evidence). That is, it is improper to hypothesize the use of a specific ignition source that has no evidence to support it even though all other hypothesized sources were eliminated.

18.7.2 Inconsistent Data. It is unusual for all data items to be totally consistent with the selected hypothesis. Each piece of data should be analyzed for its reliability and value. Not all data in an analysis has the same value. Frequently, some analysis or witness statement will provide data that appears to be inconsistent. Contradictory data should be recognized and resolved. Incomplete data may make this difficult or impossible. If resolution is not possible, then the cause hypothesis should be re-evaluated.

18.7.4 Undetermined Fire Cause. The final opinion is only as good as the quality of the data used in reaching that opinion. If the level of certainty of the opinion is only "possible" or "suspected," the fire cause is unresolved and should be classified as "undetermined." This decision as to the level of certainty in data collected in the investigation or of any hypothesis drawn from an analysis of the data rests with the investigator.

Chapter 19. Causes of Fires

19.2.1 Consideration of Data

19.2.1.1 Accidental Fire Cause. Accidental fires involve all those for which the proven cause does not involve an intentional human act to ignite or spread fire into an area where the fire should not be. When the intent of the person's action cannot be determined or proven to an acceptable level of certainty, the correct classification is undetermined. (See Section 18.6.)

19.2.1.3 Incendiary Fire Cause. The incendiary fire is one intentionally ignited under circumstances in which the person igniting the fire knows the fire should not be ignited. When the intent of the person's action cannot be determined or proven to an acceptable level of certainty, the correct classification is undetermined. (See Section 18.6.)

JURY INSTRUCTIONS

Preliminary Instruction 1—Introduction

You have been selected as jurors and have taken an oath to well and truly try this cause. This trial will last one day. During the progress of the trial, there will be periods of time when the Court recesses. During those periods of time, you must not talk about this case among yourselves or with anyone else.

During the trial, do not talk to any of the parties, their lawyers, or any of the witnesses. If any attempt is made by anyone to talk to you concerning the matters here under consideration, you should immediately report that fact to the Court.

You should keep an open mind. You should not form or express an opinion during the trial and should reach no conclusion in this case until you have heard all of the evidence, the arguments of counsel, and the final instructions as to the law that will be given to you by the Court.

Preliminary Instruction 2—Conduct of the Trial

First, the attorneys will have an opportunity to make opening statements. These statements are not evidence and should be considered only as a preview of what the attorneys expect the evidence will be.

Following the opening statements, witnesses will be called to testify. They will be placed under oath and questioned by the attorneys. Documents and other tangible exhibits may also be received as evidence. If an exhibit is given to you to examine, you should examine it carefully, individually, and without any comment.

It is counsel's right and duty to object when testimony or other evidence is being offered that they believe is not admissible. When the Court sustains an objection to a question, you must disregard the question and the answer, if one has been given, and draw no inference from the question or answer or speculate as to what the witness would have said if permitted to answer. You must also disregard evidence stricken from the record.

When the Court sustains an objection to any evidence, you must disregard that evidence. When the Court overrules an objection to any evidence, you must not give that evidence any more weight than if the objection had not been made.

When the evidence is completed, the attorneys will make final statements. These final statements are not evidence but are given to assist you in evaluating the evidence. The attorneys are also permitted to argue in an attempt to persuade you to a particular verdict. You may accept or reject those arguments as you see fit.

Finally, just before you retire to consider your verdict, I will give you further instructions on the law that applies to this case.

Final Instructions

Members of the jury, the evidence in this case has been completed, and I will now instruct you as to the law.

The law applicable to this case is stated in these instructions and it is your duty to follow all of them. Do not single out certain instructions and disregard others.

It is your duty to determine the facts, and to determine them only from the evidence in this case. You must apply the law to the facts and in this way decide the case. You must not be governed or influenced by sympathy or prejudice for or against any party in this case. You must base your verdict on evidence and not upon speculation, guess, or conjecture.

From time to time, the court has ruled on the admissibility of evidence. You must not concern yourselves with the reasons for these rulings. You must disregard questions and exhibits that were withdrawn or to which objections were sustained.

You must also disregard testimony and exhibits that the court has refused or stricken.

The evidence that you should consider consists only of the witnesses' testimonies and the exhibits the court has received.

Any evidence that was received for a limited purpose should not be considered for any other purpose.

You should consider all the evidence in the light of your own observations and experiences in life.

Neither by these instructions nor by any ruling or remark that I have made do I mean to indicate any opinion as to the facts or as to what your verdict should be.

1) Opening statements are made by the attorneys to acquaint you with the facts they expect to prove. Closing arguments are made by the attorneys to discuss the facts and circumstances in the case and should be confined to the evidence and to reasonable inferences to be drawn therefrom. Neither opening statements nor closing arguments are evidence, and any statement or argument made by the attorneys that is not based on the evidence should be disregarded.

2) You are the sole judges of the credibility of the witnesses and of the weight to be given to the testimony of each witness. In determining what credit is to be given any witness, you may consider their ability and opportunity to observe; their manner and appearance while testifying; any interest, bias, or prejudice they may have; the reasonableness of the testimony considered in the light of all the evidence; and any other factors that bear on the believability and weight of the witness's testimony.

3) You have heard evidence in this case from witnesses who testified as experts. The law allows experts to express an opinion on subjects involving their special knowledge, training and skill, experience, or research. While their opinions are allowed to be given, it is entirely

within the province of the jury to determine what weight shall be given their testimony. Jurors are not bound by the testimony of experts; the testimony of experts is to be weighed as that of any other witness.

4) The law recognizes two kinds of evidence: direct and circumstantial. Direct evidence proves a fact directly; that is, the evidence by itself, if true, establishes the fact. Circumstantial evidence is the proof of facts or circumstances that give rise to a reasonable inference of other facts; that is, circumstantial evidence proves a fact indirectly in that it follows from other facts or circumstances according to common experience and observations in life. An eyewitness is a common example of direct evidence, while human footprints are circumstantial evidence that a person was present.

The law makes no distinction between direct and circumstantial evidence as to the degree or amount of proof required, and each should be considered according to whatever weight or value it may have. All of the evidence should be considered and evaluated by you in arriving at your verdict.

5) The Court will now instruct you about the claims and defenses of each party to the case and the law governing the case. Please pay close attention to these instructions. You must arrive at your verdict by applying the law as you are now instructed to the facts as you find them to be.

The parties in this case are Flinders Aluminum Fabrication Corporation, the plaintiff, and Mismo Fire Insurance Company, the defendant. The parties have agreed, and you must regard as conclusively proven, the following facts:

a) The defendant issued a fire insurance policy to the plaintiff in January YR-10.

b) All premiums for the policy have been paid.

c) The insurance policy was in effect on November 16, YR-1.

d) On November 16, YR-1, the insurance policy covered all losses by fire up to a maximum of $10 million.

e) The aluminum fabrication plant owned by plaintiff and insured by the defendant under the fire insurance policy was destroyed by fire on November 16, YR-1.

f) The policy contains a clause that provides that the defendant will not be liable for any loss caused by or resulting from arson if that arson is the result of any deliberate acts of the plaintiff or its agents.

The plaintiff claims the fire was an accident and that it is entitled to recover $10 million from the defendant. The defendant has raised the defense of arson to plaintiff's claim.

6) The burden of proof is upon the defendant to prove the defense of arson by a preponderance of the evidence. In order for the defendant to prevail on its defense of arson, you must find that both of the following propositions have been proved:

a) The fire was caused by an act of arson.

b) The plaintiff or its agents acted deliberately to cause the fire.

If you find that either of these propositions has not been proved by a preponderance of the evidence, then your verdict must be for the plaintiff.

If you find that both of these propositions have been proved by a preponderance of the evidence, then your verdict must be for the defendant.

7) The Court did not in any way and does not by these instructions give or intimate any opinions as to what has or has not been proven in the case, or as to what are or are not the facts of the case.

No one of these instructions states all of the law applicable, but all of them must be taken, read, and considered together as they are connected with and related to each other as a whole.

You must not be concerned with the wisdom of any rule of law. Regardless of any opinions you may have as to what the law ought to be, it would be a violation of your sworn duty to base a verdict upon any other view of the law than that given in the instructions of the court.

IN THE DISTRICT COURT OF THE STATE OF NITA
DARROW COUNTY

FLINDERS ALUMINUM   )
FABRICATION CORPORATION,)
)
  Plaintiff,   )
)
  v.   )   No. CV-235894
)
MISMO FIRE INSURANCE COMPANY,)
)
  Defendant.   )

JURY VERDICT

We, the jury, return the following verdict and each of us concurs in this verdict:
(Choose the appropriate verdict.)

I

We, the jury, find for the plaintiff in the sum of $_____.

        _____
        Foreperson

II

We, the jury, find for the defendant.

        _____
        Foreperson

Special Impeachment Problems

PROBLEM 1: MARIE WILLIAMS

Assume that Ms. Williams has testified at trial on direct examination that she was never bitter or angry at Mr. Jackson, and she just wanted the best for him when their relationship terminated.

a) For Flinders, conduct a cross-examination and impeachment of Ms. Williams.

b) For Mismo, conduct a redirect examination to the extent necessary to rehabilitate.

PROBLEM 2: MARIE WILLIAMS

Assume that Ms. Williams has testified at trial on direct examination that when she confronted Mr. Jackson with her suspicions that he had hired an arsonist, Mr. Jackson looked away from her and said, "Marie, you know the trouble I'm in." Assume further that Ms. Williams testified on direct that she went to the police "immediately" after this conversation with Mr. Jackson.

a) For Flinders, conduct a cross-examination and impeachment of Ms. Williams.

b) For Mismo, conduct a redirect examination to the extent necessary to rehabilitate.

PROBLEM 3: JOHN ANDERSON

Assume that Mr. Anderson has testified at trial on direct examination that when he asked Mr. Jackson for financial information on the company, Mr. Jackson said the information had already been compiled and would be brought to the bank the next day. Assume further that Mr. Anderson testified on direct that he asked Mr. Jackson for additional collateral for the loan, but Mr. Jackson said he had no additional collateral available, that he was "tapped out."

a) For Flinders, conduct a cross-examination and impeachment of Mr. Anderson.

b) For Mismo, conduct a redirect examination to the extent necessary to rehabilitate.

PROBLEM 4: ARTHUR JACKSON

Assume that Mr. Jackson has testified at trial on direct examination that he hired Mr. Avery based upon Ms. Peterson's recommendation and after he had called Yaphank and Fass to verify Mr. Avery's achievements.

a) For Mismo, conduct a cross-examination and impeachment of Mr. Jackson.

b) For Flinders, conduct a redirect examination to the extent necessary to rehabilitate.

PROBLEM 5: ARTHUR JACKSON

Assume that Mr. Jackson has testified at trial on direct examination that he never saw or spoke to George Avery on the night of the fire, and that he saw Marie Williams as he was leaving around 6:30 p.m.

a) For Mismo, conduct a cross-examination and impeachment of Mr. Jackson.

b) For Flinders, conduct a redirect examination to the extent necessary to rehabilitate.

PROBLEM 6: ARTHUR JACKSON

Assume that Mr. Jackson has testified at trial on direct examination that at the time of the fire he was already in the process of compiling the documents the bank wanted and that he had already contacted Boeing about the plans.

a) For Mismo, conduct a cross-examination and impeachment of Mr. Jackson.

b) For Flinders, conduct a redirect examination to the extent necessary to rehabilitate.

PROBLEM 7: SONIA PETERSON

Assume that Ms. Peterson has testified at trial on direct examination that both she and Mr. Jackson checked on Mr. Avery's credentials and résumé before he was hired at Flinders.

a) For Mismo, conduct a cross-examination and impeachment of Mr. Jackson.

b) For Flinders, conduct a redirect examination to the extent necessary to rehabilitate.

Special Exhibit Problems

The following exhibit problems are designed to be used on a stand-alone basis. They create or add facts or exhibits as necessary for use in a particular exhibit foundation. **They do not add or subtract any fact or issue from the main case file, and none of the exhibit problems are to be treated as changing the main case file in any way.**

EXHIBIT PROBLEM 1

Assume that after the fire at Flinders was extinguished, and the firefighters had left the scene, Marie Williams went to the scene at 2:00 in the morning on November 17, YR-1. No one was with her. On May 20, YR-0, when Marie arrives at her deposition, she brings with her a partially melted and scorched plastic Prell shampoo bottle. There are liquid contents in the bottle, and the bottle is still intact. In black Sharpie, the initials "MW" and "11/17/YR-1—2:00 a.m." are written on the side of the bottle. Marie states that she found the shampoo bottle in the rubble on the side of the building where George Avery's office used to be. She states she opened the shampoo bottle, and it had a "funny acrid" smell that did not smell like Prell. She first put the bottle in her car for two weeks, and then she put it on a shelf in her garage until she brought it to her deposition. No one has a key to the garage except her handyman, her next-door-neighbor, and her best friend. After the deposition, the parties agree to a testing procedure for the contents of the bottle and for maintenance and preservation of the evidence, and stipulated to the accuracy of the lab's findings as to the chemical composition of the contents, but did not stipulate that the contents were present in the bottle as of November 17, YR-1. The jointly selected laboratory determined that the contents include Prell shampoo and an undetermined strong acid. Underneath the lid of the shampoo bottle, the laboratory determines that there is trace presence of hydrochloric acid.

For Mismo, offer the shampoo bottle and laboratory report into evidence. For Flinders, oppose the offer.

Exhibit Problem 2

Assume that Flinders Aluminum required all of its employees and contractors, including George Avery, to undergo fire prevention and response training. The training included a demonstration on using buckets to extinguish fires. The buckets were kept in the HCl storage room shown on Exhibit 7, approximately twenty feet from the location where George Avery's body was found on November 16, YR-1, the night of the Flinders fire. On November 17, YR-1, after the fire scene had cooled, Firefighter Henderson picked up the bucket shown next to the tape outline of George Avery's body in Exhibit 18. Henderson kept it in his evidence locker from that time until trial. Henderson will testify that the bucket was empty when he picked it up. Arthur Jackson will testify that the bucket is one of the buckets kept in the HCl storage room used in fire response training for the employees, which George Avery attended.

A) For Flinders, lay a foundation and move the introduction of the bucket into evidence. For Mismo, oppose the introduction of the bucket.

Assume that the bucket found at the scene and retrieved by Firefighter Henderson has been lost.

B) For Flinders, lay a foundation and move the introduction of a bucket that is like the bucket shown in Exhibit 18.

For Mismo, oppose the introduction of the bucket.

EXHIBIT PROBLEM 3

Exhibits 7, 8, 9, and 10 are the floor plan diagrams for the four floors of the Flinders plant. For Mismo, identify two issues/facts you would like to prove that involve the layout of the plant. Use one or more of the floor plans to assist in proving those two issues. Lay a foundation and offer the exhibit(s) and then, if admissibility is achieved, use the exhibit in some manner that helps your case. For Flinders, identify two issues/facts you would like to prove that involve the layout of the plant. Use one or more of the floor plans to assist in proving those two issues. Lay a foundation and offer the exhibit(s) and then, if admissibility is achieved, use the exhibit in some manner that helps your case. Flinders will oppose the proffer by Mismo, and vice versa. Develop all possible grounds for objection to the exhibit(s).

EXHIBIT PROBLEM 4

Assume that Flinders maintained all invoice and payment records in its Cloud account, and that the bookkeeper would simply insert an electronic "Paid" date notation on all paid invoices. In the discovery phase, Mismo Insurance Co. sent interrogatories, requests for admission, and requests for production to Flinders Fabrication, including a request for production seeking "true and accurate copies of all invoices for hydrochloric acid ordered by Flinders from 10/1/YR-2 to 11/30/YR-1." In response, Flinders produced the attached invoices from ChemGem, Inc., Nos. 10913 (Exhibit 1), 11009 (Exhibit 2), 11127 (Exhibit 3), 11323 (Exhibit 4), and 11450 (Exhibit 5). At trial, Mismo moves the admission of the invoices. Flinders objects.

A) For Mismo, establish the necessary foundation for admission of Exhibit 5, including if necessary the admission of the remaining exhibits.

B) For Flinders, make all available objections to preclude the admission of Exhibit 5 and any other offered invoices.

C) **Business records application:** For Flinders and Mismo, pick one of the invoices and establish a business record foundation for its admission into evidence; the opposing party will object to any deficiency in the business record foundation.

INVOICE 10913

CHEMGEM, INC.
Living better through chemistry

To:
Flinders Fabrication Co.
187 River Road
Nita City, NITA 99997

PRODUCT	SIZE	PRICE	QUANTITY	SHIPPED
Hydrochloric Acid	10 gal	$10.50	10	12/1/YR-2

TOTAL DUE   **$105.00**   **Payable in 30 days**

Thank you for your business!

Pd. 12/10/YR-2 #1233

1115 Industrial Plaza North
Nita City, NITA 99990
Visit out website: www.chemgen.nita

Telephone: 555-243-6436
(555-ChemGem)
Fax: 555-243-6435

EXHIBIT
1

INVOICE 11009

CHEMGEM, INC.
Living better through chemistry

To:
Flinders Fabrication Co.
187 River Road
Nita City, NITA 99997

PRODUCT	SIZE	PRICE	QUANTITY	SHIPPED
Hydrochloric Acid	10 gal	$10.50	10	3/1/YR-1

TOTAL DUE   **$105.00**   **Payable in 30 days**

Thank you for your business!

Pd. 3/6/YR-1 #1322

1115 Industrial Plaza North
Nita City, NITA 99990
Visit out website: www.chemgen.nita

Telephone: 555-243-6436
(555-ChemGem)
Fax: 555-243-6435

EXHIBIT
2

INVOICE 11127

CHEMGEM, INC.
Living better through chemistry

To:
Flinders Fabrication Co.
187 River Road
Nita City, NITA 99997

PRODUCT	SIZE	PRICE	QUANTITY	SHIPPED
Hydrochloric Acid	10 gal	$10.50	10	6/1/YR-1

TOTAL DUE   **$105.00**   **Payable in 30 days**

Thank you for your business!

Pd. 6/9/YR-1 #1382

1115 Industrial Plaza North
Nita City, NITA 99990
Visit out website: www.chemgen.nita

Telephone: 555-243-6436
(555-ChemGem)
Fax: 555-243-6435

EXHIBIT
3

CHEMGEM, INC.
Living better through chemistry

INVOICE 11323

To:
Flinders Fabrication Co.
187 River Road
Nita City, NITA 99997

PRODUCT	SIZE	PRICE	QUANTITY	SHIPPED
Hydrochloric Acid	10 gal	$10.50	10	9/1/YR-1

TOTAL DUE   **$105.00**   **Payable in 30 days**

Thank you for your business!

....
: **Pd. 9/16/YR-1 #1423** :
....

1115 Industrial Plaza North
Nita City, NITA 99990
Visit out website: www.chemgen.nita

Telephone: 555-243-6436
(555-ChemGem)
Fax: 555-243-6435

EXHIBIT
4

INVOICE 11450

CHEMGEM, INC.
Living better through chemistry

To:
Flinders Fabrication Co.
187 River Road
Nita City, NITA 99997

PRODUCT	SIZE	PRICE	QUANTITY	SHIPPED
Hydrochloric Acid	10 gal	$10.50	100	10/4/YR-1

TOTAL DUE   **$1050.00**   **Payable in 30 days**

Thank you for your business!

⋯ Pd. 10/14/YR-1 #1479 ⋯

1115 Industrial Plaza North
Nita City, NITA 99990
Visit out website: www.chemgen.nita

Telephone: 555-243-6436
(555-ChemGem)
Fax: 555-243-6435

EXHIBIT
5

EXHIBIT PROBLEM 5

Assume that on December 13, YR-1, shortly after she was fired from Flinders, Marie Williams went to the Nita General Hospital emergency room with symptoms of a panic attack. She was treated by Dr. Jill Enderight, who is no longer working at Nita General and is no longer available. Attached as Exhibit 1 is the emergency room record. Marie Williams has now sued Flinders for wrongful termination including emotional distress and pain and suffering damages.

Representing Ms. Williams for purposes of this problem, move the admission of the medical record. Call the witness or witnesses you need to admit the medical record into evidence.

For Flinders, oppose the admission.

NITA GENERAL HOSPITAL
NITA CITY, NITA

Patient: Marie Williams	MRN: 11-0667754	Location of treatment: ED
Admitted: 12/13/YR-1	Date of Discharge: 12/13/YR-1	Rx Provided: Yes
Dictated: 12/13/YR-1	Transcribed: 12/14/YR-1	Ins.: BC/BS

PHYSICIAN PROGRESS NOTES

Patient admitted to emergency department at 1623 with complaints of heaviness and tightness in chest, "racing heart," and difficulty breathing. 12-lead EKG indicates sinus tachycardia at 110 bpm. No other abnormalities in rhythm and no indication of any current or impending cardiac event. Respirations slightly elevated at 22 per minute. Temperature within normal limits. O_2 saturation 98% and normal. Blood pressure elevated at 144/98. Pt. is diaphoretic and skin is cool and pale. Pedal and radial pulses are normal and equal bilaterally.

Ms. Williams states her symptoms started during the night and worsened today, following her involuntary separation from her longtime employer, Flinders Fabrication. This pt. was last seen in ER in August YR-1, at which time she was diagnosed with a panic attack with symptoms similar to those on presentation today. At that time, pt. had been demoted, and her boss told her he was replacing her with "someone a lot more cooperative." Pt. was given therapeutic exercises to follow to assist her in responding to stressful events and was also given a prescription for Xanax prn. Pt. indicates she has obtained general relief over the past several months although her workplace has been an extremely stressful environment and her symptoms have been exacerbated at times. Her company building burned down in November.

Pt. states that her boss has now recently fired her after she accused him and a co-worker of burning down the building on purpose. Pt. states that her boss admitted the arson, but then tried to deny it, which caused pt. to be fearful and anxious. Since her firing, pt.'s symptoms have been exacerbated. Pt. was given Rx for Valium and Ambien prn. Pt. referred to her regular provider for follow-up.

/s/ Jill Enderight, MD

Certified as a true and correct copy of the original in the files of Nita General Hospital. Pursuant to N.G.S. § 47-322(A) (YR-3 Repl. Pamp.), the original of all medical records must remain in the custody of the treating hospital.

Hilda Burns
Hilda Burns
Director and Custodian, Medical Records
Nita General Hospital

EXHIBIT 1